What is the History of Knowledge?

What is History? series

John H. Arnold, *What is Medieval History?*

Peter Burke, *What is Cultural History?* 2nd edition

John C. Burnham, *What is Medical History?*

Pamela Kyle Crossley, *What is Global History?*

Pero Gaglo Dagbovie, *What is African American History?*

Shane Ewen, *What is Urban History?*

Christine Harzig and Dirk Hoerder, with Donna Gabaccia, *What is Migration History?*

J. Donald Hughes, *What is Environmental History?* 2nd edition

Andrew Leach, *What is Architectural History?*

Stephen Morillo with Michael F. Pavkovic, *What is Military History?* 2nd edition

Sonya O. Rose, *What is Gender History?*

Brenda E. Stevenson, *What is Slavery?*

Richard Whatmore, *What is Intellectual History?*

What is the History of Knowledge?

Peter Burke

polity

The right of Peter Burke to be identified as Author of this Work has been
asserted in accordance with the UK Copyright, Designs and Patents Act 1988.

First published in 2016 by Polity Press

Polity Press
65 Bridge Street
Cambridge CB2 1UR, UK

Polity Press
350 Main Street
Malden, MA 02148, USA

ISBN-13: 978-0-7456-6983-0 (hardback)
ISBN-13: 978-0-7456-6984-7 (paperback)

A catalogue record for this book is available from the British Library.

Library of Congress Cataloging-in-Publication Data

Burke, Peter, 1937–
    What is the history of knowledge? / Peter Burke. – First published in 2015
by Polity Press.
      pages; cm. – (What is history)
    Includes bibliographical references and index.
    ISBN 978-0-7456-6983-0 (hardcover : alkaline paper) – ISBN 0-7456-
6983-2 (hardcover : alkaline paper) – ISBN 978-0-7456-6984-7 (paperback :
alkaline paper) – ISBN 0-7456-6984-0 (paperback : alkaline
paper)   1. Knowledge, Sociology of–History.   I. Title.
    BD175.B8635 2015
    001.09–dc23
                                    2015016786

Typeset in 10.5 on 12 pt Sabon
by Toppan Best-set Premedia Limited
Printed and bound in the UK by CPI Group (UK) Ltd, Croydon

For further information on Polity, visit our website: politybooks.com

Contents

1 Knowledges and their Histories   1

2 Concepts   15

3 Processes   44

4 Problems and Prospects   107

Notes   126
Timeline: Studies of Knowledge, a Select Chronology   145
Further Reading   148
Index   150

For Juan Maiguashca

Remembering half a century of friendship and dialogue

1
Knowledges and their Histories

If the history of knowledge did not already exist, it would be necessary to invent it, especially in order to place the recent 'digital revolution' in perspective, the perspective of changes over the long term. At a few moments in the past, humans have lived through major changes in their knowledge systems, thanks in particular to new technologies: the invention of writing, for instance, in Mesopotamia, China and elsewhere; the invention of printing, especially block printing in East Asia and printing with moveable type in the West; and now, within living memory, the rise of computers, especially PCs, and the rise of the Internet. Changes of this kind have unpredictable consequences, both for better and for worse. As we are coming to realize in the case of the Internet, the new medium of communication offers threats as well as promises. In order to orient ourselves at a time when our knowledge systems are under reconstruction, thanks to globalization as well as to new technologies, we are well advised to turn to history.

Fortunately, the history of knowledge does exist and contributions to it are growing rapidly in number. In the early 1990s, when I began work on my book *A Social History of Knowledge*, I believed that I was more or less alone in this interest. In today's world of scholarship, however, in which the international 'republic of learning', once a few thousand strong, now contains millions of citizens, it can almost be guaranteed that if you think of a promising topic for research or an approach that seems to be new, you will soon find that other individuals and groups in different places have already had the same idea, or something rather like it. In any case, it soon became obvious that studies of the history of knowledge formed part of a trend.

It is true that until quite recently, the history of knowledge – unlike the sociology of knowledge, of which more later – was regarded as an exotic or even an eccentric topic. 'There is no history of knowledge' declared the management theorist and futurologist Peter Drucker in 1993, predicting that it would become an important area of study 'within the next decades'.[1] For once he was a little slow in his prediction, for the rise of interest in the history of knowledge was already under way at that time, including books with titles such as *Knowledge is Power* (1989), *Fields of Knowledge* (1992) or *Colonialism and its Forms of Knowledge* (1996).[2] From the 1990s onwards the history of knowledge moved from the periphery of historical interest towards the centre, especially in Germany, France and the English-speaking world. Books on the subject have been appearing more and more frequently in the last decades, as the Timeline to this book suggests, including collective studies such as *The Organisation of Knowledge in Victorian Britain* (2005).[3]

The most impressive collective study produced so far is the one in two massive volumes (with the promise of two more to come) edited by Christian Jacob, entitled 'realms of knowledge' (*Lieux de Savoir*) on the analogy of Pierre Nora's now famous 'realms of memory' (*Lieux de Mémoire*). While Nora's volumes are confined to France, Jacob's are concerned with a global history over the long term, more or less the last 2,500 years.[4]

Originally the product of a number of independent initiatives, the subject is becoming institutionalized. Academic groups for the study of the history of knowledge include one at the University of Munich and another at Oxford, both concentrating on the early modern period. Chairs have been established, including one at Erfurt University (2008) entitled 'Cultures of Knowledge in Early Modern Europe'. Centres have been founded, such as the *Max-Planck Institut für Wissenschaftsgeschichte* in Berlin (1994) and the *Zentrum*

Geschichte des Wissens in Zürich (2005).[5] There are courses in the subject, including one at the University of Manchester entitled 'From Gutenberg to Google: A history of knowledge management from the Middle Ages to the present day'. Collective projects are under way or have already been completed, among them one on the history of 'Useful and Reliable Knowledge' funded by the European Research Council.[6] Conferences on aspects of this large subject are becoming increasingly frequent. The history of knowledge is becoming a kind of semi-discipline with its own societies, journals and so on. Like knowledge itself, its history has exploded, in the double sense of rapid expansion and of fragmentation.

Historiography

Although the emergence of an organized history of knowledge is a relatively recent phenomenon, it is salutary to remember that, in past centuries, a few scholars already dreamed of a history of knowledge and even attempted to write one. In his book *The Advancement of Learning* (1605), and its longer, later Latin version, *De Augmentis Scientiarum*, the philosopher, lawyer and politician Francis Bacon expounded a plan for the reform of knowledge, an ancestor of what we now call 'science policy'. He argued that reform would be assisted by a history of the different branches of learning, discussing what was studied when and where (in what 'seats and places of learning'); how knowledge travelled, 'for the sciences migrate, just like peoples'; how it flourished, decayed, or was lost; and even what Bacon called the 'diverse administrations and managings' of learning, not only in Europe but 'throughout the world'.[7]

Three hundred and fifty years before Drucker, Bacon complained that such a history of knowledge had not yet been written. Although he inspired the 'history' (more exactly, a description) of the newly founded Royal Society written by a young clergyman, Thomas Sprat, and published in 1667, Bacon's plan was first put into practice by a number of eighteenth-century German scholars, writing what they called *historia literaria* (in the sense of a history of learning rather than a history of literature), a few decades before the rise of a self-conscious cultural history, once again produced by German scholars.[8] In France, the marquis de Condorcet, a leading figure in the Enlightenment, emphasized the growth of knowledge in his 'Sketch for an historical picture of the progress of the human mind' (*Esquisse d'un tableau historique des progrès de l'esprit humain*, 1793–1794).

In the nineteenth century, there was a movement to historicize knowledge in the sense of emphasizing its development or evolution, often viewed as 'progress'. Not only the human world but also the world of nature was now presented as subject to systematic change. This was the common message of Charles Lyell's *Elements of Geology* (1838), distinguishing different periods in the history of the earth and of Charles Darwin's *Origin of Species* (1858), organized around the idea of evolution via natural selection. Karl Marx argued that what people know and what they think is the result of their position in society, their social class, while the philosopher-sociologist Auguste Comte was interested in the history as well as in the classification of the different disciplines and tried to persuade the French minister of education to establish a chair in the history of science (he failed).

In the early twentieth century, the history of science that Comte had advocated was introduced in some universities, especially in the USA. German-speaking scholars established what they called the 'sociology of knowledge' (*Wissensoziologie*), concerned with who knows what and with the uses of different kinds of knowledge in different societies, in the past as well as in the present.[9] The history of the natural sciences has been taken as a model for other histories: the history of the social or 'human' sciences, the history of the humanities, and finally the history of knowledge in general. In German, it is possible to speak of a shift from the more academic *Wissenschaftsgeschichte* to the more general *Wissensgeschichte*.[10] In English, we might call it a shift from the history of the sciences to the history of knowledge.

This shift is quite recent. Why should this be? Changes in the present have often prompted historians to look at the past in new ways. The study of environmental history, for instance, is driven by debates about the future of the planet. In similar fashion, current debates about our 'knowledge society' or 'information society' have encouraged an historical approach to the topic.[11] Historians have made only a relatively small contribution to the general discussion, less than they could or should have made, since one of the social functions of historians is surely to help their fellow-citizens to see the problems of the present in a long-term perspective and so to avoid parochialism.

Parochialism in space is well known: a sharp division between Us, the members of one's community, and Them, everyone else. However, there is also parochialism in time, a simple contrast between 'our' age and the whole of an undifferentiated past. We need to try to escape this limited view, in this case to see the digital revolution that we are experiencing today as the latest in a whole series of knowledge revolutions. A few historians have responded to this challenge, the challenge of historicizing the knowledge society.[12] One scholar has written about what he calls the 'early Information Society' of eighteenth-century Paris, while two others have claimed that 'Americans have been preparing for the Information Age for more than three hundred years.'[13]

We shall return to the problem of continuity and revolution in Chapter 4. Here it may be sufficient to note that the history of knowledge has developed out of other kinds of history, two in particular. The first is the history of the book, which has developed in the last few decades from an economic history of the book trade to a social history of reading and a cultural history of the spread of information.[14] The second is the history of science, where the turn to a broader history of knowledge has been driven by three challenges.

One challenge is a consequence of the awareness that 'science' in the modern sense of the term is a nineteenth-century concept, so that to use the term about knowledge-seeking activities in earlier periods encourages what historians hate most, anachronism. The second challenge has come from the rise of academic interest in popular culture, including the practical knowledges of artisans and healers. The third and most fundamental challenge has come from the rise of global history and the consequent need to discuss the intellectual achievements of non-Western cultures. These achievements may not fit the model of Western 'science', but they remain contributions to knowledge.

What is knowledge?

To sum up so far, the last few decades have seen what might be described as an epistemological turn, both inside and outside the academy. This collective turn, like other turns in the humanities and social sciences (the linguistic turn, the visual turn, the turn to practice and so on), raises a number of awkward questions. The most obvious of these questions is What is knowledge? A philosophical question, but one that historians of knowledge cannot simply abandon to the philosophers, who in any case disagree. For one philosopher, for instance, knowledge is any state in an organism that bears a relationship to the world.[15]

Before trying to answer this question, it is worth noting that some historians, especially in the USA, prefer to speak about 'information', as in the case of books like *A Nation Transformed by Information* or *When Information Came of Age*.[16] In similar fashion, two sessions at the American Historical Association's annual conference in 2012 were entitled 'How to write a history of information' and 'Secret state information'. The choice of the term 'information' rather than 'knowledge' illustrates the empiricist culture of the USA, contrasting in particular with the German concern for theory and *Wissenschaft*, a term often translated into English as 'science' but referring more widely to different forms of systematically organized knowledge.

In my view, both terms are useful, especially if we distinguish between them. 'We are drowning in information', we are sometimes told, but 'starved of knowledge'. In his play *The Rock* (1934) T. S. Eliot already asked the questions, 'Where is the wisdom we have lost in knowledge?' and 'Where is the knowledge we have lost in information?' Borrowing a famous metaphor from Claude Lévi-Strauss, it may be useful to think of information as raw, while knowledge has been cooked. Of course, information is only relatively raw, since the so-called 'data' are not objectively 'given' at all, but perceived and processed by human minds that are full of assumptions and prejudices. However, this information is processed again and again in the sense of being classified, criticized, verified, measured, compared and systematized, as Chapter 3 will illustrate. In what follows distinctions will be made between knowledge and information whenever this is necessary, although the term 'knowledge' will sometimes be used to refer to both elements, especially in the titles of chapters and sections.

Some scholars have focused on the history of belief (in French, *histoire des croyances*), generally concentrating on religious belief. Believers, on the other hand, consider their beliefs to be knowledge. As for historians, they are well advised to extend the concept of knowledge to include whatever the individuals and groups they are studying consider to be knowledge. For this reason, beliefs are not discussed separately in this book.

Knowledges in the plural

Despite the title of this study, it might be argued that there is no history of knowledge. There are only histories, in the plural, of knowledges, also in the plural. The current explosion of the history of knowledge makes this point all the more obvious – as well as making an attempt to fit the pieces together all the more necessary. Hence this book will follow the example of Michel Foucault, who often wrote of *savoirs* rather than a single *savoir*; the management theorist Peter Drucker, who suggested that 'We have moved from knowledge to knowledges'; and the anthropologist Peter Worsley, who declared that 'there are knowledges, not simply Knowledge with a capital K'.[17]

Even within a given culture, there are different kinds of knowledge: pure and applied, abstract and concrete, explicit and implicit, learned and popular, male and female, local and universal, knowing how to do something and knowing that something is the case.

A recent study of the scientific revolution of the seventeenth century contrasted 'what was worth knowing' in 1500 and in the eighteenth century, emphasizing the shift from 'knowing why' to 'knowing how'.[18] What is considered worth knowing varies a good deal according to place, time and social group. So does what is taken for granted: the doctrine of the Trinity, for instance, the efficacity of witchcraft or the roundness of the earth. Equally variable is what counts as the justification for belief: oral testimony, written evidence, statistics and so on. Hence the recent rise of the phrase 'cultures of knowledge' or *Wissenskulturen*, including practices, methods, assumptions, ways of organizing and teaching and so on.[19] The phrase is a helpful one, provided that we remember that different knowledges may coexist, compete and conflict within a given culture: dominant and subjugated knowledges, for instance, as a recent study by Martin Mulsow of the clandestine circulation of unorthodox ideas in eighteenth-century Germany reminds us.[20]

Even the concept of knowledge varies with place, time and above all with language. In ancient Greek, there was a division of labour between *techne* (knowing how), *episteme* (knowing that), *praxis* (practice), *phronesis* (prudence) and *gnosis* (insight). In Latin, a distinction was made between *scientia* (knowing that) and *ars* (knowing how), while *sapientia* (derived from *sapere*, 'to know') meant wisdom, and *experientia* referred to knowledge derived from experience. In Arabic, *episteme* was translated as *'ilm* (plural *'ulum*, 'the sciences', so that scholars used to be known as the *'ulema*). The equivalent of *gnosis* was *ma'rifah*, and the equivalent of *sapientia* was *hikma*.[21] In China, *zhi* meant knowledge in general, while *shixue* referred to knowhow.

In German, a distinction has developed between *Erkenntnis* (knowledge from experience, formerly *Kundschaft*) and *Wissenschaft* (academic knowledge). In English, the words 'scientist' and 'expert' both emerged in the early nineteenth century, a time of increasing specialization. So did a word for the knowledge possessed by ordinary people: 'folklore', often implying an inferior form of knowledge. In French, the best-known distinction is that between *savoir*, a general term for knowledge, and *connaissance*, referring to specialized knowledges. In similar fashion, different groups of knowledgeable people have been described in French as *intellectuels* (who play a public role), *savants* (who are mainly academics) and *connoisseurs* (who know about art or wine).

Conflicts between different kinds of knowledge have often arisen. When Milan cathedral was under construction at the beginning of the fifteenth century, for instance, a dispute between the local master masons and the French architect in charge of the project was formulated in terms of the relative importance of practical knowledge (*ars*) and theory, especially geometry (*scientia*). In the seventeenth century, professional physicians ridiculed the practical knowledge of midwives and unofficial healers. In the late eighteenth century, a French miller went into print to criticize the 'doctors', in other words the *savants*, for their arrogance in presuming to tell millers and bakers how to do their jobs.[22]

As a result of these variations and conflicts, there has been much work on the history of knowledge in these different senses and there remains still more to do. Books have been published about practices such as observing and describing and attitudes such as objectivity. If any kind of knowledge is timeless, it is surely wisdom, but as I write, a forthcoming book is announced concerned with its history, or perhaps with the history of what has been thought to be wisdom in different places over the centuries.[23]

History and its neighbours

A plain or general historian who sets out to study the history of knowledges soon becomes aware that valuable contributions to this subject have already been made by scholars coming from a variety of disciplines, close and more distant neighbours. For this reason a brief discussion of what have been described as 'academic tribes and territories' is in order, so as to insert the research conducted by historians into a bigger picture.[24]

Unsurprisingly, many disciplines take knowledge as an object of study as well as their goal. The neighbours of the history of knowledge include sociology, anthropology, archaeology, economics, geography, politics, law and the histories of science and philosophy (further away is the multidisciplinary field of cognitive studies, to be discussed in Chapter 4). Communities beyond the university must not be forgotten either. Archivists, librarians and the curators of museums have all made valuable contributions to what we might call 'knowledge studies'.

Of these neighbouring tribes, the closest is the history of science, which has moved from a focus on the great ideas of great scientists to the study of institutions such as scientific societies, of practices such as experiment and observation and of places such as laboratories and botanical gardens. A number of contributions to the history of knowledge might be described as history of science (of this new kind) under another name. Philosophy is another close neighbour. From the ancient Greeks onwards, philosophers have been concerned with epistemology (from the Greek term, *episteme*), asking questions such as What is knowledge? How do we come to know anything? Is our knowledge reliable? One leading figure in the renewal of epistemology was Michel Foucault, who moved from philosophy to the history of medicine and from studies of madness and clinics to more general reflections on the relation between knowledge and power (*savoir* and *pouvoir*), including the lapidary statement that 'The exercise of power perpetually creates knowledge and conversely, knowledge constantly induces effects of power.'[25] Francis Bacon, who knew that knowledge empowers, or, as he put it, 'enables' government, while governments manage knowledge, could not have made the point more succinctly.[26]

The social factors that influence knowledge, or what is considered to be knowledge in a particular milieu, have long been the concern of sociologists. In the 1920s, in the first wave of what was coming to be known as the 'sociology of knowledge', Mannheim launched the idea of the 'existential binding' or 'situational binding' (*Seinsverbundenheit, Situationsgebundenheit*) of thought, in other words the 'affinity' between 'thought-models' and 'the social position of given groups'. This idea was a milder or more open version of Karl Marx's claim that thought was determined by social class. As Mannheim wrote, 'By these groups we mean not merely classes, as a dogmatic type of Marxism would have it, but also generations, status groups, sects, occupational groups, schools, etc.'[27]

From the 1970s onwards, a second wave of the sociology of knowledge became visible.[28] In important respects, the contributions of Pierre Bourdieu to the sociology of knowledge continued Mannheim's work. Bourdieu studied the French university system or, as the author called it, the academic 'field' or 'battlefield', analysing the conditions of entry and the relation between individual positions in the field and different strategies and forms of academic power. Mannheim had praised scholars who had the courage to subject their own point of view, as well as that of their adversaries, to social analysis. Bourdieu actually wrote what he called 'reflexive sociology', turning his penetrating gaze on his own work and that of his colleagues as well as on the natural scientists.[29] Meanwhile, the so-called 'Edinburgh School' of the sociology of science put forward what they called a 'strong programme' that attempted to go beyond Mannheim and explain successful theories in the natural sciences as well as unsuccessful ones.[30]

The idea of situated knowledge was itself situated. Mannheim, for instance, was a young man at the time of the outbreak of the First World War and the collapse of the Austro-Hungarian Empire in which he had grown up, a collapse that led many people to question beliefs that they had formerly taken for granted. The second wave of the sociology of knowledge, from Foucault to Bourdieu, followed the famous 'events' of May 1968 in Paris, when students not only fought the police in the streets but also questioned the academic system. At much the same time, the rise of feminism encouraged the analysis of the obstacles to the careers of female scholars and, more positively, of studies of female 'ways of knowing', to be discussed in Chapter 4.[31] A third element in the situation in the 1970s was the rise of 'postcolonial' thinkers, responding to the process of decolonization – or, more exactly, to the perceived limitations of that process. Offering a case-study of the relation between power and knowledge in the style of Foucault, Edward Said argued that Western studies of 'the Orient' were essentially a means of dominating that region.[32]

The work of Pierre Bourdieu, who studied Algeria before he studied France, may equally well be described as contributing to the sociology or the anthropology of knowledge. Once upon a time the two disciplines were relatively distinct. Sociologists studied whole societies and they offered explanations of what they described in terms of varieties of social structures. Anthropologists, by contrast, did their fieldwork in villages and offered cultural explanations of what they observed, including what they used to describe as 'ethnoscience'. Just as linguists recorded endangered languages before they died out, anthropologists, especially the group calling themselves 'cognitive anthropologists', recorded what might be described as 'endangered knowledges', including the knowhow of builders, smiths and carpenters. The idea of knowledges or 'cultures of knowledge' in the plural, like the idea of cultures in the plural, came from anthropologists. One of the leading figures in anthropology today, the Norwegian Fredrik Barth, has devoted much of his long career to studies of knowledge in different societies ranging from Bali to New Guinea.[33]

More recently, the differences between sociology and anthropology have become blurred. Bruno Latour, for instance, a French scholar who straddles anthropology and the history of science and plays a leading role in Science and Technology Studies, has carried out 'fieldwork' in laboratories (a biochemical laboratory in his case), in order to observe scientific knowledge in the making, thus placing Western science on the same footing as the knowledge of peoples such as the Trobrianders, say, or the Azande, both of whom were the subject of classic anthropological studies in the 1920s and 1930s. Latour went on to produce what he called an 'ethnography' of the French supreme court, the *Conseil d'État*. This cheeky move by anthropologists raises a major problem to which Chapter 4 will return, the problem of relativism.[34]

Archaeologists are interested in the reconstruction of knowledge and ways of thought in 'prehistoric' times, in other words before the invention of writing systems. Attempting to infer knowledge and thought from material remains, they have turned towards anthropology, since many anthropologists have studied societies similar to those of prehistoric times, small in scale and using simple technologies. Hence 'cognitive archaeology' runs parallel to cognitive anthropology, making use of the findings of cognitive science in the search for the 'ancient mind'.[35]

The emphasis on the sites in which knowledge is produced, visible in the work of Foucault, has inspired geographers as well as historians.[36] In this discipline too, a recent epistemological turn has become visible. It may be illustrated by a recent study of geographies of scientific knowledge, inspired by the paradox that scientific knowledge is, (or at least claims

to be), universal, yet it is produced in particular environments, such as laboratories, and (at least predominantly) in
particular cultures.[37]

Economists have long been interested in the role of information in economic decisions, but from the 1960s onwards
a 'cognitive turn' in parallel to other disciplines became
visible, discussing knowledge as a form of capital. The Japanese management theorist Ikujiro Nonaka, for instance, has
argued that the 'knowledge-creating company' is more innovative and so more competitive. Some economists treat
knowledge as a commodity that can be bought and sold, even
though, as one theorist admits, 'it is difficult to make information into property'.[38] This last process is the domain of
the lawyers. The law of intellectual property, sometimes
known as IP, is one of the fastest-growing sections of the law
in the USA, in the European Union, and elsewhere, in response
to the problems of copyright in a range of new media as well
as to disputes over patents.[39]

Departments of politics or political science, on the other
hand, have made less of a contribution to knowledge studies
than might have been expected. It was left to an outsider,
Michel Foucault, to make the famous statement, quoted
above, about the relation between power and knowledge.
Again, the phrase 'geopolitics of knowledge' is associated not
with a specialist in geopolitics but with a professor of literature, Walter Mignolo, while introductions to geopolitics have
little to say about knowledge, even though they discuss topics
such as maps and public opinion.[40]

In similar fashion, although information is obviously as
crucial to political and military decisions as it is to economic
ones, students of politics have largely left it to sociologists,
geographers and historians. One distinguished exception to
this rule is Roxanne Euben, Professor of Political Science at
Wellesley College, who has compared travel in search of
knowledge in the Islamic and Western worlds in her *Journeys
to the Other Shore* (2006). Another is James C. Scott, Professor of Political Science and Anthropology at Yale University,
whose book *Seeing Like a State* (1998) offers a critique of
the general and abstract knowledge that underlies planning
by central governments, and makes a plea for what the author
calls 'practical knowledge', 'embedded in local experience'.[41]

It is surely no accident that interest in local knowledge is often linked to a concern with imperialism and subjugated or subaltern knowledges and that it is strongest today in what used to be called the 'Third World', especially Africa and South America. In Bamako in Mali, for instance, a Centre for Research on Local Knowledge has been founded, while Spanish American scholars who discuss the topic include Walter Mignolo and Luis Tapia.[42]

Just as studies of memory have expanded to include the complementary opposite topic of forgetting, knowledge studies are coming to include studies of ignorance, including knowledge that has been lost or consciously rejected (below, Chapter 2).[43] Needless to say, the author of this book also suffers from ignorance. My own knowledge of knowledge is patchy, to say the least. I know much less about the rest of the world than about the West, about knowledges outside the university than about academic knowledges, and about the natural sciences than about the humanities. Despite these limitations, what follows will attempt to show something of the variety of histories of knowledges. It begins with key concepts, moves on to the processes that turn information into knowledge that can be disseminated more widely and used for different purposes, and concludes by discussing recurrent problems and future prospects in this field.

2
Concepts

The recent rapid expansion of knowledge studies in general and of the history of knowledge in particular has led to the proliferation of new concepts. We are faced with what virtually amounts to a new language – not to say 'jargon' – so much so that something like a glossary is becoming necessary. As a first step in this direction, what follows will discuss a small group of terms that help us not only to read and write about the history of knowledge but to think about it as well.[1] As in the case of glossaries, items will be arranged in alphabetical order.

Authorities and monopolies

As studies of colonial situations suggest, knowledges may be plural but they are not equal: that is, they are not treated as equal. Some individuals, groups and institutions (the Church, the state or the university, for instance) are 'authorities', in the sense that they have the power to authorize or reject knowledges, to declare ideas to be orthodox or heterodox, useful or useless, reliable or unreliable, indeed to define what counts as knowledge or science in a particular place and time.[2]

The example of the Inquisition is too well known to need more than a brief reference, like the example of authoritarian states such as Stalin's Russia or Hitler's Germany, but it may be worth lingering for a moment on the case of universities, analysed at length (in the case of Paris in the 1960s) in a classic study by Pierre Bourdieu.[3] Some academics, known in Italian as 'barons' (*baroni*), may be described as 'gatekeepers' who control appointments, access to research funds and even entry to a given intellectual field, whether they make their decisions on the basis of intellectual merit, 'correct' views, or membership of the baron's patronage network. Other scholars, described by Bourdieu as 'the consecrated heretics', concentrate on their research and acquire international prestige, but exercise little power in the world of the universities.[4]

With unexpected tact, Bourdieu omitted the names of individual academics from his analysis, but it is not difficult to fill in at least some of the blanks. One famous example of an academic baron in Paris in the 1960s was the historian Roland Mousnier, professor at the Sorbonne and an opponent of both the Marxists and the historians of the so-called '*Annales* School', whose aim was to write a new kind of history, with less emphasis on politics than had been customary and more emphasis on the economy, society and culture. Fernand Braudel, leader of the *Annales* group, was another baron, charismatic and authoritarian, a visionary and an empire builder. Professor at the Collège de France, outside the university system, Braudel might be described as one of Bourdieu's 'consecrated heretics'. However, he did have a power base in the VIth section of the Ecole des Hautes Etudes and also in the Maison des sciences de l'homme, an interdisciplinary institute that he founded. Braudel combined the gift of spotting talent with the power to make or break careers, while his alliance with another professor at the Sorbonne, Ernest Labrousse, who supervised a record number of doctoral dissertations (42 in all), allowed him to influence the younger generation.[5]

Long before Bourdieu, an anonymous Victorian satirist encapsulated the idea of academic power in a quatrain put into the mouth of a leading academic baron of the time, Benjamin Jowett, a leading classicist and Master of Balliol College Oxford.

> I come first, my name is Jowett,
> All that's knowledge, well I know it,

What I don't know isn't knowledge.
I'm the Master of the College.

Some authorities, notably clerical elites such as the Catholic priesthood and the Muslim *'ulama*, have attempted to establish monopolies of knowledge, or at least of its most prestigious forms in a given culture. According to the Canadian economic historian Harold Innis, each medium of communication has tended to create a monopoly of knowledge. Innis regarded these monopolies as extremely dangerous. In compensation, they were vulnerable to competition from other media, so that 'the human spirit breaks through' from time to time. The intellectual monopoly of medieval monks, for example, based on parchment, was undermined by paper and print, just as the 'monopoly power over writing' exercised by Egyptian priests in the age of hieroglyphs had been subverted by the Greeks and their alphabet. In the case of Innis, it is difficult to resist the suspicion that the economic historian's interest in competition, in this case between media, was reinforced by the Protestant's critique of 'priestcraft' (Innis had planned to become a Baptist minister before turning to an academic career).[6]

Curiosity

Curiosity, the impulse to know, may appear to be a constant feature of human psychology, but attitudes to that impulse, as well as the meaning of the term 'curiosity' and its equivalent in other languages (*curiositas* in Latin, *curiosità* in Italian, *Curiosität* in German, and so on), have changed a good deal over the centuries. Although Aristotle approved of curiosity, as one might have expected, given the wide range of his studies, other ancient writers emphasized its dangers. In the early Christian centuries, Ambrose criticized Cicero for believing that astronomy and geometry were worth knowing, while Augustine regarded curiosity as a vice, associated with pride. For many Christians, the story of Eve and the apple was a warning against the perils of female curiosity in particular.

Medieval philosophers were torn between the positive view of Aristotle and the negative view of Augustine. It was only at the Renaissance that we find a 'rehabilitation' of curiosity, a return to Aristotle's positive view, while Francis Bacon put forward the idea of 'an essential human right to knowledge'.[7] Even then, the story of Dr Faustus selling his soul to the devil in return for knowledge (among other things) reminds us that the negative view of curiosity still had adherents. It may have been as late as the Enlightenment that the positive view became dominant, symbolized by Kant's motto, 'dare to know' (*sapere aude*, a quotation from the Roman poet Horace).

To complicate the story, as Neil Kenny has shown, the meanings and associations of terms such as 'curious' in English, French, German and other languages were (as they still are) multiple and changeable. In the seventeenth century, these meanings ranged from 'careful' to 'elegant' and from 'inquisitive' to 'odd'. Only the context tells us that the *collegium curiosum* founded at Altdorf in 1672 was meant to refer to a club of lovers of knowledge, especially experiment, rather than to a group of eccentrics.[8] 'Cabinets of curiosities', known in German as 'cabinets of marvels' (*Wunderkammer*), in other words the private museums that became fashionable in early modern Europe, contained objects that provoked wonder because they were strange, rare, made with unusual skill or perceived as 'exotic' because they came from distant places.

The rise of the idea of 'useful knowledge' in the eighteenth century implied a new critique of knowledge for its own sake, a critique that was worldly rather than religious. In the English Royal Society, for instance, the mathematicians opposed the election of Joseph Banks as President because they feared that he would turn the Society into 'a cabinet of trifling curiosities'.

Disciplines

In Chapter 1, a distinction was made between 'information' that is relatively raw, and knowledge that has been processed or 'cooked'. A more formal name for this process of testing, elaboration and systematization is 'scientification'. This word still sounds somewhat ponderous in English as well as evoking the natural sciences at the expense of the humanities, although its German original, *Verwissenschaftlichung*, has a wider application, to society as well as to knowledge, and has come to be generally accepted. Scientification is often, if not always, an elaboration of everyday practices such as observation, description and classification, making them more precise but at the same time more remote from the experience of ordinary life. The process is sometimes called 'disciplining' (in German: *Disciplinierung*). It is central to the formation of academic disciplines.

Like the idea of discipline in athletics, religion and war, the concept of an intellectual 'discipline' is an old one, emphasizing the ascetic side of the scholar's career as well as the need for a kind of apprenticeship until the necessary skills have been internalized. We might describe a discipline as a set of intellectual practices that are distinctive (or, at least, believed to be distinctive) and that are institutionalized in professions such as law or medicine. Academic disciplines have sometimes been compared to nations. They have their own traditions and territories, their 'fields' and their frontiers, warning trespassers to keep out (the term intellectual 'field' (*campus*) can be found in Cicero, and again in early modern scholars such as Johannes Wower, author of *De polymathia* (1603), but it only became common in the nineteenth and twentieth centuries).[9]

Systems of disciplines vary with the orders of knowledge of which they form a part. The best-known system of disciplines, and one that has come to dominate the intellectual world, is the Western one, despite the fact that, as a recent study emphasizes, 'none of the basic activities that each discipline comprises is confined to Europe or even just to "advanced" industrial societies across the world'.[10]

In the nineteenth century, academic disciplines and fields multiplied at a vertiginous rate. Their autonomy took physical form in departments, separated by a location in different buildings or by walls or floors of the same building. The university became an archipelago, a collection of more or less independent intellectual islands. It has become difficult, though not impossible, to move from one island to another, as the sections on interdisciplinarity and intellectuals will suggest.

Innovation

Although universities used to be essentially concerned with
preserving and transmitting knowledge, creating new knowledge has been one of their main functions ever since the rise
of the research university in the nineteenth century. Firms too
search for new knowledge in order to improve their products
and outstrip their competitors, and encouraging innovation
is one of the principal tasks of knowledge managers.

Contributions to the theory of innovation have come from
a whole range of disciplines, among them economics (Joseph
Schumpeter), sociology (Vilfredo Pareto), geography (Torsten
Hägerstrand), psychology (Liam Hudson), urban studies
(Richard Florida) and management (Ikujiro Nonaka). Might
historians also have something to offer?

In the first place, studying traditions of knowledge, historians are likely to suggest that what is generally recognized
as innovation will often turn out, if analysed more closely,
to be an adaptation for new purposes of an earlier idea or
technique. In short, innovation is a kind of displacement.
What makes these displacements happen?

One answer to this question, offered by the Dutch scholar
Anton Blok, focuses on the kinds of people who innovate.
Blok offers a strong, provocative argument to the effect that
people who become famous as innovators do not have more
talent than their colleagues, but they do work harder, indeed
obsessively so. They behave in this way because they have
had to contend with difficulties, often from early childhood
(loss of parents etc). Innovators, Blok argues, are usually
outsiders, geographically (they are provincials), psychologi-
cally (they are loners), socially and intellectually. They take
more risks than their established colleagues because they
have less to lose.[11]

An alternative approach focuses on groups rather than
individuals. Although the mythology of innovation is dominated by individual geniuses, recent studies suggest that the
propensity to innovate is a collective as well as an individual
phenomenon, depending on interaction and exchange. The
most important milieu for creative interaction is a small
group, usually a face-to-face group, especially a group that

meets regularly. Ideally, this group should be composed of people with common interests but different approaches, often linked to differences in their education, in different countries or in different disciplines. Displaced ideas often come from displaced people (below, Chapter 3).[12]

How can such groups be encouraged? In the past, they were often encouraged by the growth of cities. Cities are magnets for immigrants from different places and with different skills and they offer niches or spaces of sociability such as taverns and coffeehouses where discussion can flourish, producing the 'buzz' that leads to new ideas. Our problem today is that the increasing size of cities makes it more difficult for different kinds of people to meet.

Intellectuals and polymaths

A history of knowledge is necessarily concerned with different kinds of knowledgeable people inside and outside the university. A concept that recurs in discussions of knowledgeable people is that of 'intellectual', principally in the sense of a writer or scholar who speaks out on public issues. A well-known example is that of the novelist Emile Zola at the time of the notorious 'Dreyfus Case' in France (1894–1906). Zola led the group that argued that Captain Dreyfus, who had been charged with treason for divulging military secrets to the Germans, was in fact innocent. It was in this context that the French word 'intellectuel', which later spread to many languages, was originally coined.[13] An earlier and more precise term is 'intelligentsia', originally a Russian word referring to writers and scholars who opposed the authoritarian regime of the tsars.[14]

Another species of knowledgeable person is the expert or the 'specialist', a term coined in the mid nineteenth century, originally in a medical context, at a time when medical specialisms were multiplying.[15] The term soon came to be used more widely. A very different species is the scholar familiar with a number of different disciplines, the polymath or the 'generalist' as the American scholar Lewis Mumford (best known as an architectural critic and a student of cities) liked to describe himself. The term 'polymath' came into regular use in the seventeenth century, at a time when scholars were already beginning to be worried by the fragmentation of knowledge, although a few remarkable individuals were still able to make original contributions to a number of different fields. Gottfried Wilhelm Leibniz, for instance, is now remembered as a philosopher, but he also made discoveries in mathematics, history and linguistics.

Since the eighteenth century, following the rise of more and more specialist knowledges, polymaths have often been regarded as an endangered species. They have never become extinct, although they have become less ambitious. It may be useful to distinguish two types of wide-ranging scholar. One is the passive polymath, such as the writer Aldous Huxley, who is said to have read the *Encyclopaedia Britannica* from cover to cover but made no significant contribution to knowledge himself. The other is the serial polymath, who is trained in one field and later moves to others.

Two well-known examples of serial polymaths are Michael Polanyi and Jared Diamond. Polanyi, a political refugee first from Hungary and then, in 1933, from Germany, was a professor of physical chemistry who turned philosopher, writing about the 'tacit knowledge' discussed later in this chapter. Diamond was a physiologist who moved into ornithology but is probably most widely known today for his books on world history, *Guns, Germs and Steel: The Fates of Human Societies* (1997) and *Collapse: How Societies Choose to Fail or Survive* (2005). Their universities have been quite accommodating to these changes of fields. Polanyi simply moved from the department of chemistry to the department of philosophy at the University of Manchester, while Diamond transferred from a chair in physiology to a chair in geography at the University of California at Los Angeles.[16]

Interdisciplinarity

Serial polymaths are in a particularly good position for practising interdisciplinarity, in other words taking ideas or methods current in one field and employing them in another. Interdisciplinarity may be regarded as a necessary antidote to specialization. Like the division of labour in general, specialization increases efficiency and so contributes to the growth of knowledge. At the same time what has been called 'knowing more and more about less and less', or even 'knowing everything about nothing', has sometimes proved to be an obstacle to new discoveries and new theories.[17] Living on islands in the academic archipelago encourages intellectual insularity. Hence the continuing need to avoid the intellectual 'frontier police', as Aby Warburg, a private scholar best known for his contributions to the study of images, memory and the classical tradition, used to say.

The twentieth century was a time of many attempts to institutionalize interdisciplinarity by means of informal discussion groups like the History of Ideas Club at Baltimore in the 1920s (bringing together philosophers, historians and literary scholars), or more formally by the foundation of organizations such as the *Institut für Sozialforschung* (Institute for Social Research) at Frankfurt in 1923. Some of these organizations have ambitious aims, like the Institute for the Unity of Science in The Hague (founded in 1936), while others are relatively modest, like the centres of 'area studies' founded in the USA with government assistance, largely for political reasons, in the age of the Cold War. The best-known of these institutions is probably the Russian Research Center founded at Harvard in 1947, in which economists and sociologists worked with historians and political scientists, focusing on the USSR.

Knowledge management

'Knowledge management' is a relatively new phrase that spread in the 1990s, when courses on the subject were founded in a number of fields, from business to librarianship. A *Journal of Knowledge Management* was founded in 1997. An associated idea is 'science policy', a concern of governments and also an object of academic study (the Science Policy Research Unit at the University of Sussex was founded in 1966). The phrase 'knowledge management' is also associated with the concept of 'intellectual capital', viewing information and ideas as a resource or investment that needs to be protected and used wisely. Hence the appointment of Chief Knowledge Officers and Chief Information Officers (CKOs, CIOs) in many firms, also from the 1990s onwards.

Ensuring that the information stored on the firm's computers is secure from hacking has become an increasingly important part of their job.

All the same, the story of knowledge management did not begin in the 1990s. The future of knowledge has often been planned and to a lesser extent shaped by individuals in strategic positions outside the academic world. In the seventeenth century, Francis Bacon, Lord Chancellor, had a vision of collective research, requiring an organizer or co-ordinator, while the 'information master' Jean-Baptiste Colbert, King Louis XIV's minister of finance, 'amassed enormous libraries and state, diplomatic, industrial colonial and naval archives; hired researchers and archival teams; founded scientific academies and journals; ran a publishing house; and managed an international network of scholars'.[18] In the eighteenth century, Joseph Banks was active as a kind of knowledge manager, combining his official position as President of the Royal Society with an unofficial but powerful role as adviser to King George III.[19] In the nineteenth century, a leading knowledge manager was Friedrich Althoff, a civil servant in Berlin with considerable influence over the appointment of professors and the foundation of research institutes.[20]

In the twentieth century, Warren Weaver, director of the Division of Natural Sciences at the Rockefeller Foundation, 1932–55, funded projects in genetics, agriculture and medicine and supported the emerging discipline of molecular biology (as he named it) at a decisive moment. On the side of the humanities and social sciences, Shepard Stone, Director of International Affairs at the Ford Foundation, gave money for research to the Free University of Berlin, St Antony's College Oxford and the Institute for European Sociology in Paris, not only to advance knowledge but to fight Communism and improve the image of the United States abroad.[21]

Knowledge society

Awareness of the need for knowledge management is a response to the rise of the so-called 'knowledge society' or 'information society', a subject of debate by economists, sociologists and management theorists from the 1960s onwards. Economists such as Fritz Machlup noted the increasing numbers of 'knowledge workers'. Sociologists such as Daniel Bell argued that 'industrial society' had been succeeded by 'post-industrial society'.[22] Management theorists suggested that knowledge, which they described as 'intellectual capital', made companies more innovative and so more competitive.[23] In the digital age, the rise of the knowledge society accelerated. It has been argued, for instance, that capitalism was restructured in the late twentieth century thanks to changes in information technology.

The knowledge society is generally regarded as something quite new, not only by journalists and the general public but also by sociologists such as Manuel Castells, who has written about what he calls the 'information age'.[24] On the other hand, as we saw in Chapter 1, the few historians who have intervened in this debate have tended to stress continuity. Indeed, a Dutch historian has written about the medieval 'knowledge economy' as part of what he calls the 'long road' to the Industrial Revolution.[25]

There is an obvious need to avoid two opposite dangers: on one side the simplistic contrast between the present and an undifferentiated past, and on the other an exaggerated emphasis on continuities. To quote the American historian Robert Darnton, 'every age was an age of information', but 'each in its own way'.[26] What we need to do is to distinguish these ways: the age of manuscript, for instance, from c.3000 BCE onwards, and the first age of print and paper, running in the West from 1450 to 1750 or thereabouts. After 1750, periodization becomes more difficult and controversial, but we might distinguish five more ages: the age of statistics, 1750–1840; the age of steam and electricity, 1840–1900 (conveying information by the steam press, steamship, railway and telegram); the age of Big Science, 1900–50; the age of three revolutions, 1950–90 (the third age of discovery, third scientific revolution and third industrial revolution); and our own age, the Age of the World Wide Web, from around 1990 onwards.[27]

Orders of knowledge

One of the fundamental concepts in the history (or the sociology or the anthropology) of knowledge is that of 'orders of knowledge', 'orders of learning' or 'orders of information'. Foucault, provocative as usual, claimed that 'each society has its regime of truth' as well as using the less controversial phrase 'orders of knowledge'.[28] These orders are often defined by place (Western, Islamic, and East Asian, for instance) or by period (medieval, modern, and perhaps post-modern). For example, the book that you are reading now has been written from within the British variety of the Western order of knowledge in an age of transition from the ascendancy of print to digital dominance.

The essential point is that the main forms and institutions of knowledge to be found in a particular culture, together with the values associated with them, form a system: schools, universities, archives, laboratories, museums, newsrooms and so on. The connections between different parts of the system are probably most visible to outsiders, while insiders take the whole order for granted. The orders are not planned but they are shaped by the values of the culture as well as by interactions between organizations founded for specific purposes.

In traditional China, for instance, the system was dominated by Confucianism and the civil service examinations. In the Ottoman Empire, the order of knowledge was dominated by Islam and more specifically by the mosque schools or *medreses*. In the USSR, it was dominated by Marxism and by the Academy of Sciences. Since the knowledge order is part of the larger socio-cultural order, it is no surprise to discover the importance of central control and the dominance of Paris in the twentieth-century French order of knowledge, in sharp contrast to the decentralized system of the United States.

Today, it is becoming increasingly implausible to speak of a single dominant order. In Britain, for example, we see competition between the BBC and its rivals, between different churches and mosques, between different kinds of school and university, and so on, not to mention the increasing use of international search engines online.

In other words, orders of knowledge change, even if the rate of change tends to be slow. European universities reacted only gradually to the rise of printed books, while lectures remain a staple mode of disseminating academic knowledge to this day.[29] Again, in the North American order there has been a gradual change in the balance of power between institutions, with the rise of the university to 'ascendancy' in the production of knowledge in the late nineteenth century, followed by its decline a century later, as both public and private research institutes or 'think tanks' became an increasingly important part of the scene.[30]

Alternatively, information orders might be defined by the means of communication dominant in a given place or time: oral, written, printed or digital, bearing in mind that when each new medium arrives it does not replace but rather coexists with all the earlier ones. Competition between media often settles down into a division of labour like the one between manuscript and print in early modern Europe, where manuscripts retained importance not only for clandestine communication but also for the circulation of poems and other works by nobles who associated print with the commerce they often despised.[31]

The concept of orders of knowledge underlies recent comparative studies of what we now call 'science' in early modern Europe, China and the world of Islam.[32] A penetrating example of this comparative approach is Geoffrey Lloyd's study of ancient Greece and China, in which he notes that, in the study of nature, the Chinese had an advantage over the Greeks, government support, while the Greeks had an advantage over the Chinese, a tradition of discussion and dispute.[33]

Without the concept of order, or something like it ('system', 'culture' or 'regime'), comparisons between knowledges in different places, different periods or different social groups would be difficult indeed. Another advantage of the concept is to warn us against false analogies. For example, a given practice, such as healing the sick or writing about the past, even if it is similar in certain respects in different cultures, may still occupy a different place in each of them. Simplifying somewhat, one might say that in ancient Rome history was written by senators for senators, while in early medieval Europe it was written by monks for monks and today, by professors for students. It is hardly surprising that the questions asked about the past and the answers given to them have changed a good deal over the centuries.

On the other hand, the concept of a knowledge order raises problems as well as solving problems. If we divide the world into orders according to geography, should we speak of the Western order (as opposed to the Islamic or East Asian), or the French order (as opposed to the English or the American)? The great problem is that of frontiers. 'Systems' are not watertight (or, in this case, 'information-tight'). Frontiers of knowledge, like the one between the world of Christendom and the world of Islam in the sixteenth century for instance, have generally been porous, since many people travelled while at least some travellers were open to ideas from outside. If some degree of movement and openness were not the case, intellectual change would be limited, if not impossible – yet we know that it happens, often on a massive scale.

Another disadvantage of the concept of order of knowledge is that it implies a homogeneity that does not exist. Viewed more closely, an order fragments into dominant knowledges and subordinate ones that are often perceived by elites either as heretical or, in the case of popular knowledges, dismissed as unworthy of attention. In the Ottoman empire, for instance, the dominant order, that of the *'ulama* (in Turkish, *'ulema*) was challenged by that of the Sufis, mystics who prized *ma'rifah* rather than *'ilm* (above, Chapter 1).[34] In China, the Confucian order of knowledge was challenged by Buddhists and Daoists. In short, the concept of an order of knowledge is useful on condition that we recognize that it represents a kind of intellectual shorthand, a helpful simplification of a more complex reality.

Practices

'Practice' has become a central concept in studies of knowledge, beginning with studies of the history of reading and the history of experiment, spreading to analyses of observation, note-taking and description, and summed up in the two massive volumes edited by Christian Jacob, *Lieux de Savoir*, described by the editor as contributions to 'the history and the anthropology of intellectual practices'. The crucial point here is the awareness that habits that seem timeless are in fact subject to change, even if the changes are gradual and generally imperceptible. An important everyday intellectual practice is classification. Classifications differ between cultures and disciplines, but in a given culture or discipline they may appear to be natural, a tendency that Foucault encouraged his readers to question, notably in his famous description, borrowed from the Argentinian writer Jorge Luis Borges, of a Chinese encyclopaedia that divided animals into fourteen categories that included 'those that belong to the emperor', 'embalmed ones' and 'those drawn with a fine camel-hair brush'.[35] Although this Chinese encyclopaedia never existed, anthropologists have found almost equally surprising contrasts with Western ways of classifying in their examination of 'folk taxonomies', the ways in which the different peoples of the world name colours or arrange plants, animals and birds. A well-known study with the provocative title, 'Why is the cassowary not a bird?' analysed the logic of the zoological taxonomies of the Karam, a people living in the highlands of New Guinea, explaining that the Karam thought of cassowaries as family members.[36]

Intellectual practices also include the more or less formal procedures for acquiring, classifying or testing knowledge, such as dissecting bodies, observing stars through a telescope, conducting experiments and so on. Some of these are characteristic of a particular discipline (like diagnosis in medicine), while others (such as comparison) are common to a number of disciplines. Yet others (note-taking, for example) are even less formal and still more widespread. Each of these practices has a history, in the sense of changing over the long term.[37] The fact that scientific methods have often if not always developed out of less formal everyday practices is one more reason (besides the desire to avoid ethnocentrism and anachronism) for incorporating the history of science in a broader history of knowledges.

Professionalization

The rise and multiplication of different disciplines has sometimes been regarded from a purely intellectual point of view, as a response to the increasing accumulation of knowledge, especially from the nineteenth century onwards. However, the story has a social aspect as well. Sociologists use the term 'professionalization' to refer to a process that includes not only the multiplication of full-time occupations, each with its own kind of knowledge, but also the establishment of bodies that make the rules governing entry to a particular occupation, organize training, maintain collective standards and so on.[38] Thus healers turn into physicians organized in colleges, while PhDs become necessary for careers in the academic world. Professional organizations tend to become bureaucratic, in the sense of spelling out the rules for entry, awarding diplomas, adopting formal procedures for appointment, promotion, the funding of projects and so on.

Take the case of nineteenth-century Britain, when the old professions (the Church, the law, medicine, the army and navy) were joined by a number of new ones: engineering, architecture, accounting, surveying, teaching and so on. In Britain, the Society of Engineers (founded in 1824) was joined by the Institution of Surveyors (1868) and the Institute of Chartered Accountants (1880).

The process of professionalization is accompanied by the development of a technical language or occupational jargon, facilitating communication within the group at the same time as rendering it more difficult when insiders speak to outsiders). A professional ethos develops: pride in one's occupation, which may be viewed as a calling rather than simply a means of making a living, together with loyalty to one's colleagues.

As in the case of 'knowledge order', discussed above, the concept of professionalization has costs as well as benefits. It directs attention to what is common in the rise of different professions at the expense of attention to differences. It fits newer professions, like accountant, better than old ones, like medicine, and it fits the more practically useful occupations better than the humanities.[39]

Take the opposite cases of librarians and historians. To speak of the professionalization of librarians is relatively unproblematic. Libraries used to be managed by scholars, as in the famous case of the polymath Gottfried Wilhelm Leibniz at the ducal library in Wolfenbüttel. Now they are managed by librarians who have been to library school and belong to a professional association. In the United States, for instance, the American Library Association was founded in 1876 and the first library school was established soon afterwards by Melvil Dewey.[40] International conferences are another indicator of professionalization and the first international congress of archivists and librarians took place in 1910. On the other hand, it is more difficult to say when some historians turned professional. There is an argument for choosing the mid nineteenth century, taking the famous example of Leopold von Ranke and his pupils in Berlin, Munich and elsewhere in the German-speaking world. This was the time when historians could find full-time employment in universities or in archives. However, the role of official historian has a much longer history in Europe, going back to the fifteenth century if not before. In any case, for some early modern scholars, history was already viewed as a 'calling'.[41] The foundation of the American Historical Association in 1884 may have made historians more conscious that they formed a group with its special interests, but it was far from the beginning of professionalization.[42]

The idea of professionalization is linked to that of expertise. The rise of the words 'expert' and 'expertise' took place in Britain in the nineteenth century, their first use being recorded in 1825 and 1868 respectively. The new terms are linked to a new trend, the increasing reliance by governments on specialist advice on practical problems such as sanitation, town planning or the management of the economy. John Maynard Keynes, for instance, was a Cambridge economist who advised the government after the Great Depression of 1929, joining the Economic Advisory Council in 1930.[43]

Regimes of ignorance

The concept of an order of knowledge surely requires including its complementary opposite, the organization of non-knowledge or ignorance. In fact some scholars have begun to study what they call 'regimes of ignorance', in other words what is not known by different kinds of people in certain places or times.[44]

Anthropologists have studied secrets and secret societies in some West African cultures, for instance, while economists have made analyses of decision-making by firms in conditions of uncertainty. Sociologists have emphasized the paradox that 'non-knowledge', like silence, is a resource that has its uses, at least in certain circumstances. The anonymity of examination candidates, for example, encourages fairness in the examiners.[45] On the other side, the dangers of ignorance may be illustrated by governments that pursue economic growth or technological change without knowing what the long-term impact of their policies on the environment and so on society will be over the long term.

Historians have not published many studies of ignorance so far, although they sometimes offer examples of its historical importance, for example when one group attributes ignorance to another, thus justifying imperial rule. In the case of the French Revolution, the problem of the 'control of the definition of ignorance' has been discussed; 'the ability to brand others as ignorant and thereby disqualify them from a voice in the affairs of the city', in Marseilles for instance. Again, a study of the use of statistics by the German state notes the fact that in 1920, in the crisis of transition from the German Empire to the Weimar Republic, 'the vacuum of knowledge' about the state of the German economy 'was almost complete'.[46]

All the same, it is not difficult to imagine what might be done in the future, most obviously in the history of empires. In recently conquered territories, for example, conquerors usually knew little about the resources of the lands that they had taken over, or about the cultures of the inhabitants. Surveys made by the Spaniards in the New World, by the British in India or by the French in North Africa might be viewed in negative as well as positive terms as more or less successful attempts to plug these holes in the knowledge that was essential to the efficient exercise of power. In these empires, military and political decisions as well as economic ones were taken in conditions of particular uncertainty and sometimes led to disaster.[47] From the point of view of the conquered peoples, on the other hand, the ignorance of their masters was a valuable resource.

Situated knowledges

Karl Marx had already written about the way in which thought, especially what he called 'ideology', was shaped by society and its social classes. Offering a milder version of Marx's claim, Mannheim, as we saw in Chapter 1, described knowledge as 'tied' to everyday life, situated in a particular time, place and community. Historians of knowledge therefore need to place or more exactly replace it 'in context'. This is the aim of the Society for Social Studies of Science (1975), as it is of the journal *Science in Context* (1987).

Where Mannheim thought of social situation mainly in terms of class and generation, later scholars extended the concept further. The American scholar Donna Haraway wrote a famous essay on 'situated knowledge' in which she discussed situation in terms of gender. For his part, Michel Foucault viewed situation in terms of place, especially the micro-spaces, such as clinics, factories and prisons, in which knowledge is produced or employed. Indeed, in an interview conducted by geographers, he once admitted to what he called 'spatial obsessions'.[48] In similar fashion the French Jesuit Michel de Certeau, who was, among other things, an historian, published an essay claiming that written history was 'the product of a place', in other words the result of a set of social, political and cultural conditions that make some kinds of research possible and others impossible.[49] This essay may have inspired the collective study of *Lieux de Savoir* that was mentioned in Chapter 1.

In the wake of Foucault and Certeau, many scholars have turned to the study of the sites or, as Bacon called them, the 'seats' of knowledge, small or large. Some focus on a building such as a clinic or a laboratory, in which particular intellectual practices take place.[50] Others are concerned with cities such as Rome, Paris or London, viewed as networks of smaller sites (universities, libraries, monasteries, coffeehouses and so on).[51]

Another group of studies emphasize the 'geopolitics of knowledge', especially the relation between intellectual centres and their peripheries. According to a powerful if

simplistic model, this relation resembles the economic relation between a metropolis – usually if not always a Western
metropolis – and its colonies. The places described by Bruno
Latour as 'centres of calculation' (Paris, for example, or
London) import the raw material of information from the
periphery, and export the finished product, knowledge, in
return.[52] Different kinds of knowledge had different centres
at different times. In the eighteenth century, for instance, the
university city of Uppsala became a centre for botanical
knowledge thanks to the presence of Carl Linnaeus.

The centre–periphery model can obviously be criticized as
Eurocentric. It has often been assumed that the spread of
knowledge has been one-way, from the West to the 'rest',
despite the many examples of movement in the opposite
direction, to Europe from the Islamic world or from China.
Again, the model assumes that what the West imported was
raw information, although it can be shown that some Europeans in India, China and elsewhere also took over indigenous systems of classification (of plants, for instance). In the
third place, the model treats the knowledge that moved as if
it did not change in transit, although what was imported was
translated into different languages and adapted to different
circumstances.[53]

It might also be useful to modify the model by introducing
the notion of 'semi-periphery', thinking of colonial cities such
as sixteenth-century Goa or eighteenth-century Calcutta
where an important part of the work of translation, adaptation and even publication took place.

Styles of thought

The idea of different modes of thinking is a topic that has
been discussed by philosophers for centuries, using terms
such as *manière de penser* or *Denkungsart*. In the 1920s, it
became an object of sociological and historical study. In
France, Marc Bloch's *Les rois thaumaturges* (1924) discussed
the practice of the French and English kings of touching suf-
ferers from scrofula in order to heal them. What most interested Bloch was the way in which the belief in the royal
power to heal survived all the evidence to the contrary. He

later studied the history of medieval 'ways of thinking' (façons de penser) more generally, turning away from the great ideas of great thinkers and directing attention to the everyday ideas of ordinary people.[54]

In Germany, the sociologist Karl Mannheim distinguished between different 'styles of thought', as he called them, characteristic of different periods and different nations, noting, for example, the contrast between the French 'liberal-universal' and the German 'conservative-historicist' styles in the early nineteenth century.[55] Almost simultaneously and apparently independently, the Polish biologist Ludwik Fleck used the identical term 'style of thought' (Denkstil) to distinguish between what he called different 'thought collectives', defining such a collective as 'a community of persons exchanging ideas'. Fleck pointed out that one's own style of thought (like one's own point of view) seems natural and necessary, while any other style seems odd or arbitrary.[56]

In the 1950s, the German sociologist Heinrich Popitz and the Polish sociologist Stanisłas Ossowski both argued that the social structure is perceived differently by individuals located at different points within it. Pierre Bourdieu went further still in this direction by noting that these differences in perception included those of sociologists themselves.

Subjugated knowledges

The division of intellectual labour between centres and peripheries is a reminder of the need to expand the concept of situation to include encounters between cultures, or rather, encounters between individuals and groups from different cultures, each with their own knowledges. Encounters include conquests, producing colonial situations in which knowledges coexisted on unequal terms. The knowledges of the conquerors became dominant, while local knowledges were 'subjugated'. These subjugated knowledges were often forgotten or at least unacknowledged by members of dominant groups, as in the case of individuals from the West who wrote about or mapped the non-Western world but had little to say about what they had learned from indigenous informants.[57]

A famous and controversial case-study, inspired by Foucault, of the role of knowledge in the domination of the

Middle East by the West (especially the French and British governments) is *Orientalism* (1978), written by the Palestinian-American critic Edward Said. Said defined orientalism as at once an academic specialism, 'a body of knowledge in the West'; a 'style of thought'; and finally, as a 'corporate institution' supporting Western dominance.[58] This dominance began with Napoleon's invasion of Egypt in 1798, when the French army was accompanied by 167 scholars in a commission for sciences and arts. Their collective research culminated in the publication of a multi-volume *Description de l'Egypte* (1809–28).[59]

Said's account is a landmark in studies of the Middle East and extremely critical of earlier studies in the field. It has often been criticized in its turn for reducing Western interest in 'the Orient' to the desire to dominate, neglecting the scholars who were driven by disinterested curiosity, as scholars often are.[60] Take the case of the Englishman Edward William Lane, who spent many years in Egypt between 1825 and 1849, learned Arabic, dressed as an Egyptian, and published his *Manners and Customs of the Egyptians* in 1836. According to Said, Lane's book contributed to 'academic Orientalism', which in turn contributed to Western dominance. This negative judgement is in sharp contrast to that of Lane's biographer Leila Ahmed, who suggested that he described Egyptian culture and society 'in the terms in which a member of that culture experienced them'.[61]

For another example of subjugated knowledges we might take India in the age of rule by the East India Company (1757–1857) and then by the British government (1858–1947). The contribution of knowledge, or more exactly of a variety of knowledges, both indigenous and Western, to British rule in India was obvious enough to the rulers themselves. Two hundred years before Foucault's remarks on power and knowledge, the Governor-General of Bengal, Warren Hastings, declared that 'Every accumulation of knowledge and especially such as is obtained by social communication with people over whom we exercise dominion … is useful to the state.'

Knowledge has been the central theme of a number of important studies of British India which combine a concern with the macro-level, the collision between two orders of knowledge, and a concern with the micro-level, encounters between individual Britons and Indian informants. The Cambridge historian Christopher Bayly, for instance, emphasized the debt of the British to the 'information order' of the Mughal rulers into whose shoes they stepped. The American anthropologist Bernard Cohn distinguished a number of what he called 'investigative modalities', forms of enquiry such as travel, surveys, surveillance and the collection of statistics. In this unequal encounter between two epistemological regimes, the British, in Cohn's words, 're-ordered' Indian knowledge.[62] It might be more exact to say that knowledge was re-ordered by Indians, working as guides, translators, spies or clerks, and incorporating Western information into their own order or orders of knowledge, as well as by the British, whether they tried, like missionaries, to transform Indian knowledge, or, as administrators, to incorporate information from indigenous informants into their own system.[63]

In short, the British production of knowledge about India was really a joint production, the result of a dialogue between different groups, 'though not always in equal measure'.[64] It might be useful to think about this situation in terms of cultural negotiation. 'Negotiation' is a somewhat elusive concept, but it might be described as a semi-conscious process of response to the ideas of another person or group, a partial appropriation and incorporation of those ideas. In this sense, negotiation should be distinguished from conscious attempts by both missionaries and indigenous scholars to reconcile Western science with Indian traditions, both Hindu and Muslim.

Tacit knowledge

Intellectual innovation develops not only from interaction between disciplines but also from outside the academic system, from practical knowledge or 'knowhow'. Orders of knowledge include practical, tacit or implicit knowledges, 'knowing how' to do something, as opposed to 'knowing that' something is the case, the form of knowledge dominant in the academic world. Michael Polanyi, the serial polymath mentioned earlier, made his contribution to epistemology by arguing that 'we can know more than we can tell', offering a variety of examples of skills that are difficult to put into words and have to be learned in practice, skills ranging from riding a bicycle to diagnosing illness or tasting wine.[65] It would be easy to add to this list: playing the violin, making furniture, cooking, boxing, connoisseurship (dating and attributing works of art) and so on. Polanyi's 'tacit knowledge' can also be described as embodied knowledge, as it was by one of the leading analysts of knowledge in the late twentieth century, Pierre Bourdieu.

Bourdieu liked to speak of 'habitus', an old concept but one that he developed with characteristic brilliance, describing a set of skills and assumptions that have been so well internalized that individuals are no longer aware that they possess them, whether they are footballers or physicists. A particular habitus allows someone to improvise within a framework of unconscious or semi-conscious rules.[66] True to form, Bourdieu studied his own practice, describing it as the result of a 'cleft habitus', a conflict between his upbringing in a peasant community in South West France and his later training as a philosopher, anthropologist and sociologist. He also argued that a habitus 'was not a destiny', but capable of being transformed by experience.[67]

Studying embodied practices of tacit knowledge poses serious problems for historians. Take the case of the crafts, the many products of what is sometimes called the 'mindful hand' or 'vernacular epistemology'.[68] Artisanal knowledge is literally handed down (the original meaning of 'tradition') from master to apprentice by example, almost without words. Hence the study of the crafts depends on fieldwork and participant observation, methods that are impossible to follow in the study of the past.

For example, a British anthropologist Trevor Marchand carried out his 'fieldwork' as an apprentice to a master builder in Yemen, helping to construct minarets, and noting that the master 'found it tremendously difficult to "explain" *what* he knows, or, more importantly, *how* he knows'. Learning the craft involved a regular exchange between master and apprentice of the roles of observer and performer.[69] In a later study of woodworkers in London, however, Marchand noted that observing and performing were assisted by brief explanations in words. This observation implies that, unlike Polanyi, we should think in terms of more or less tacit knowledges rather than drawing a sharp distinction between tacit and explicit.[70]

It is no surprise to find that this part of the history of knowledge has been neglected, at least relatively speaking. What is not put into words is rarely recorded, so that it is difficult to find sources for the study of changes in these practices over the long term. It is also difficult to interpret the sources once they have been discovered. Hence the historian Pamela Smith collaborated with a silversmith to reconstruct the techniques described in a sixteenth-century French manuscript on metal-working.[71]

However, it is sometimes possible to observe tacit knowledges in the process of becoming explicit thanks to textualization, especially the rise of how-to-do-it books that began to proliferate in the generation after Gutenberg and flourish to this day – books about book-keeping, dancing, farming, writing letters, horsemanship and more recently child-rearing, management, and so on. Indeed, it has been argued that the so-called 'scientific revolution' of the seventeenth century was the fruit of an encounter between the explicit and tacit knowledges of scholars and artisans. Scientific experiments, for example, were an elaboration of the 'trial and error' techniques that were common practice on the part of goldsmiths, for instance.[72] We might speak of the new knowledge produced in this way as 'hybrid' or 'translated'.

Tools of knowledge

Practices are both supported and shaped by material culture, especially by what have been called 'tools of knowledge'. For example, the practices of observation associated with the 'scientific revolution' of the seventeenth century depended on new scientific instruments, especially two: the telescope and the microscope. Today, some kinds of scientific research depend on enormous tools such as the Herschel Space Telescope or the Large Hadron Collider in Geneva, built to assist the study of particle physics.

Medium-size tools include blackboards, filing cabinets, microscopes, personal computers, and in early modern times celestial and terrestrial globes and the book-wheels that made it easier for scholars to view two or more open books at once. 'Little tools of knowledge' should not be forgotten, including simple things such as pens, inkwells, blotting paper, carbon paper, record cards and paper clips.[73] Think too of the special walking-stick carried by the philosopher Thomas Hobbes. Thoughts often came to Hobbes while he was walking and he needed to record them. But how could he write them down when away from his desk? According to his friend John Aubrey, Hobbes always carried a notebook with him. He also 'had in the end of his cane a pen and ink-horn' so that no thoughts would be lost.

Traditions

As in the case of arts and crafts and other forms of knowhow, the academic production of knowledge generally follows traditions as well as sometimes breaking them.[74] Historians can scarcely do without the notion of tradition, although they might be well advised to abandon what might be called the traditional notion of tradition, in other words a cluster of practices and modes of thought (whether explicit or tacit) handed down (in Latin, *tradere*) from one generation to the next.

The problem here, as in the case of the idea of the 'transfer' of knowledge from one place to another, is the assumption that what is transferred remains the same. It was in reaction against this false assumption that Eric Hobsbawm put forward his famous idea of the 'invention of tradition', originally formulated to describe some cultural movements in Europe between 1870 and 1914, and later extended much more widely by other scholars.[75] However, to speak of 'invention' is also problematic, since it implies beginning with a blank slate. It is usually more exact to say that traditions are revived, reconstructed or translated in order to fit changing situations, new needs, or, in the case of traditions of knowledge, new discoveries. In the case of the classical tradition, the German scholar Aby Warburg was already practising this approach in the 1920s.[76]

Traditions are often viewed in a negative way, as so many obstacles to innovation. On the other hand, there are milieux and moments in which the oxymoron 'traditions of innovation' seems to be appropriate. Take the case of the French historians known collectively as the '*Annales* School', a group that has survived for four generations, beginning with the founders, Marc Bloch and Lucien Febvre; continued by Febvre's intellectual heir, Fernand Braudel, and his colleague the economic historian Ernest Labrousse; succeeded by a third generation, including the medievalist Jacques Le Goff; and continued in the fourth generation by Roger Chartier, Bernard Lepetit and others.[77] Each generation learned from the previous ones, but each generation developed a distinctive approach, with individual variations.

Despite the claims to universal knowledge on the part of natural scientists, it has been argued that particular styles of thought and practices of research form part of national traditions as well as disciplinary ones.[78] Anglo-American empiricism has often been contrasted with the German emphasis on theory. In the humanities, 'four ways' of practising anthropology have been studied, respectively British, German, French and American.[79] In the case of the history of knowledge itself, three regional traditions (in a broad sense of the term 'region') have been particularly influential. The German tradition stems from the sociology of knowledge as practised by Mannheim and others, and draws on the work of German philosophers. The French tradition draws on the sociologist Emile Durkheim as well as on Foucault. The Anglo-American tradition has emerged from the history of the natural sciences. Even today, when many major works produced in all three traditions have been translated, differences of approach remain visible in the ways in which knowledge is gathered and elaborated, processes that will be discussed in the following chapter.

Translating knowledges

The spread, transfer or dissemination of knowledge has often been discussed. Scholars used to assume that what was disseminated remained more or less the same as it moved from place to place or from person to person. Today, on the other hand, the opposite assumption has become dominant, in other words the idea that what arrives differs in important respects from what set out. It is mediated. Propositional knowledge ('knowledge that') needs to be translated into different languages in order to travel, but concepts that are central in one language may be lacking in others, as missionaries to China, for instance, found when they attempted to translate the Christian idea of 'God'. Hence the need for 'negotiation'. Indeed, one might say that translation is a kind of negotiation, while negotiation is a kind of translation.[80]

Translation between languages offers particularly clear examples of the problems of what is known as 'cultural translation', in the sense of the adoption and consequent adaptation to one culture of items originating in another. A given 'culture of knowledge', large or small, forms a system, and if a new item is introduced into the system it is virtually bound to be modified, even if, in the longer term, the system is modified as well. Cultural 'transplantation' is followed by cultural 'transformation'.[81] In short, following a model involves a certain degree of innovation.

Conversely, what is generally recognized as innovation will often turn out, if we analyse it more closely, to be an adaptation of an earlier practice or institution – a free or creative adaptation, but an adaptation nonetheless. In similar fashion, it has been suggested that new ideas come into being by extending or 'displacing' old ones.[82] Thinking of innovation as displacement draws attention to the role of 'displaced people'.

One kind of displaced person is the exile or refugee, like the Greeks who fled West as the Ottoman Empire expanded in the fifteenth century, the Protestants who left Catholic countries in the sixteenth and seventeenth centuries or the Jewish intellectuals who participated in what has been called the 'Great Exodus' from Germany and Austria in the 1930s. The refugees took their intellectual capital with them, as in the case of the 'skill migration' of Protestant silk-weavers from France to London, Amsterdam and Berlin.

Looking for a job in their new home, other exiles turned to translation, a form of mediation between their former culture and their new one. In the United States in the mid twentieth century, for instance, German-speaking refugees introduced the ideas of philosophers such as Nietzsche, psychologists such as Freud and sociologists such as Max Weber. They translated texts into English, and they also engaged in 'cultural translation', explaining foreign ideas in terms that members of the host culture would understand. The result was a kind of hybridization, most obviously between the American tradition of empiricism and pragmatism and the German tradition of theory, incorporated in the Institute for Social Research at Frankfurt, mentioned above, which was transferred to New York, after Hitler came to power, and later migrated to California.[83]

Another kind of migrant intellectual might be described as a 'nomad' or a 'renegade'. Academic nomads or renegades are individuals who were trained in one discipline but migrate to another, taking along with them the habitus of the old discipline but applying or adapting it to the new. Vilfredo Pareto, for instance, was trained as an engineer and carried over ideas from engineering, notably the concept of equilibrium, into the studies of economics and sociology. Again, Robert Park, a leading member of the Chicago School of sociology, was active as a newspaper reporter before he entered academic life. He carried with him the habit of investigative reporting, turning it into sociological 'fieldwork' in the city. Both Pareto and Park may be described as translators between disciplines.[84]

Equipped with this conceptual tool-box, we may turn in the following chapter to the many processes that information undergoes as it is turned into knowledge, disseminated in different places among different social groups and employed for a variety of purposes.

3
Processes

Having presented some concepts in the previous chapter, it is time to use them to examine the career of items of information as they are discovered, analysed, 'cooked' or 'processed' and so transformed into knowledge. The variety of disciplines is linked to the variety of practices, although specific disciplines rarely monopolize a given practice. Borrowing from one discipline to solve problems in another will be a recurrent theme of what follows, as it is of intellectual history in general. This chapter is organized around a sequence of practices, different stages in the process of making and using knowledge. As we have seen, the process of making can be described in German in a single word, *Verwissenschaftlichung*, sometimes translated as 'scientification' but not limited to the natural sciences, so that 'systematization' might be a more exact rendering. It is all too easy to assume that these systematizing practices are unchanging. In fact, as scholars increasingly emphasize, they are time-bound, pursued according to different rules and with different kinds of support in different epochs and milieux.[1] What follows offers a series of examples illustrating the historicity of these procedures.

Attempting objectivity

The problem of the variety and the irreconcilability of human points of view is an old one. One attempt at a solution is known as 'objectivity', which might be described as an attempt to separate knowledge from the knower and thus to present a 'view from nowhere'. This collective attempt reached its peak over a hundred years ago, before sociologists of knowledge, from Mannheim onwards, began to undermine it. As Lorraine Daston and Peter Galison have recently shown, 'Scientific objectivity has a history.'[2] To be precise, objectivity has several histories, since the story differs in the natural and the social sciences, not to mention the history of history itself.

In the natural sciences, the stress on objectivity, defined as 'blind sight, seeing without inference, interpretation, or intelligence' had its heyday in the 1860s and 1870s. Photography was at once a means to this self-effacement of scientists in the service of science and an inspiration for it. The pioneer photographer William Fox-Talbot, in his *Pencil of Nature* (1844), praised the new technology precisely because the images 'have been formed or depicted by optical and chemical means alone, and without the aid of any one acquainted with the art of drawing'. In short, they are 'impressed by Nature's hand'. In the twentieth century, by contrast, leading scientists came to emphasize the place of intuition in discovery and the value of trained judgement.

In the case of history, in the seventeenth and eighteenth centuries, the ideal was 'impartiality', otherwise known as freedom from 'bias'. It was in the nineteenth century that historians borrowed the language of scientific objectivity, bending it to their own purposes, notably the attempt to avoid expressions of national prejudice. The cosmopolitan Lord Acton, general editor of the *Cambridge Modern History* (1902), provided a famous formulation of the ideal (while employing the traditional language of 'impartiality') in letters to Cambridge University Press and to the contributors, telling them that 'Our scheme requires that nothing shall reveal the country, the religion, or the party to which the writers belong' and that 'our Waterloo must be one that satisfies French and English, Germans and Dutch alike'. In the 1930s, however, two leaders of the profession in the USA, Carl Becker and Charles Beard, argued that objectivity in historical writing was impossible, no more than a 'noble dream'.[3]

Newspapers also claimed to be impartial. For example, the *London Courant* of 1688 promised to present information 'with the integrity of an unbiased historian', 'representing things as they shall really happen'.[4] The ideal was sometimes expressed in the title of the paper, as in the case of *The Impartial Reporter*, founded in Ireland in 1825. By the twentieth century, the claim was made in the language of objectivity. In the United States in the 1920s, for instance, 'objectivity became a fully formulated occupational ideal, part of a professional project or mission'.[5]

Another way of thinking about the relation between investigators on one side and the cultures that they investigate on the other is to employ the language of the sociologist Norbert Elias and oppose 'involvement' to the 'detachment' that Karl Mannheim (with whom Elias had worked in Frankfurt) believed to be characteristic of what he called the 'free-floating intellectual' (*freischwebende Intelligenz*). In the case of historians, attempts at 'distance' from the past have been contrasted with efforts to come close to it. These attempts and efforts have their own history.[6] In the nineteenth century, Leopold von Ranke and his followers (including Lord Acton) tended to view the past from a distance, while Jules Michelet and Thomas Carlyle identified themselves with some historical events and their protagonists.

Four stages

It is convenient to distinguish four main stages in the sequence that runs from acquiring information to using it: gathering, analysing, disseminating and employing, although it will be useful to introduce further distinctions later. Needless to say, the four categories are fluid rather than fixed. Observation, for instance, is not only a means to understand but requires previous understanding in order to be effective. If, say, individuals from Anglo-Saxon England were to visit London today, it would be difficult for them to make sense of much of what they saw.

Although both gathering and analysis are indispensable, analysis has generally had more prestige. In the nineteenth century, mathematics and philosophy were often considered to be 'higher' pursuits than natural history because they were analytical while natural history was only descriptive. Analysis was also contrasted with 'the mere gathering of raw facts'. Indeed, some scientists believed that 'all the physical sciences aspire to become in time mathematical'. In similar fashion, the Victorian polymath Herbert Spencer declared that sociology stood to history 'much as a vast building stands related to the heaps of stones and bricks around it', and that 'The highest office which the historian can discharge is that of so narrating the lives of nations, as to furnish materials for a Comparative Sociology.'

Gathering Knowledges

The acquisition of information includes 'gathering' in the literal sense of collecting plants for medical or botanical purposes, collecting rocks as geological 'specimens', and so on. These material objects are as near to raw 'data' as one can get, but even here the gatherers operate with principles of selection shaped by their culture. In other words, the process of transformation from 'raw' to 'cooked' has already begun. A similar point about selection can be made still more strongly about other forms of collecting information, by historians studying documents, journalists interviewing politicians and so on. In these cases there is a double filter, since the politician or the author of the historical document selected the information from which the journalist or the historian made another selection, each for their own purposes.

For many centuries, individuals have travelled in search of knowledge. In Arabic, a special phrase exists to describe this kind of travel, *talab al-'ilm*, and a saying attributed to Muhammad is often quoted: 'Seek knowledge, even as far away as China.' The fourteenth-century historian Ibn Khaldun pointed out that learning was revived in the Maghrib thanks to individuals who travelled to centres of learning such as Baghdad and Damascus and returned to transmit what they had learned. Still more ambitious was the fourteenth-century Moroccan Ibn Battuta, who took Muhammad's recommendation literally and made his way to China.[7]

Within Europe, medieval students, the wandering scholars, moved from one university to another. The custom, known as *peregrinatio academica*, continued into the early modern period and has of course been revived in our own time. In the twentieth century, scholars travelled in order to conduct 'fieldwork', whether to collect botanical or geological specimens or, in the case of anthropology, to study different cultures at close hand. Historians too travel in order to gather knowledge, whether they visit archives or, in the case of oral history, interview informants and record their memories of past events and processes.

As those last examples suggest, gathering knowledge is not limited to picking flowers or picking up shells but extends to observation, asking questions or more generally listening to what people say.

Observing

Observation is more than simple looking. It might be described as close looking, a practice penetrated by ideas if not by theories. It comes in a number of varieties, techniques learned in different situations by different kinds of people for different purposes, from astronomers gazing at the stars to physicians offering diagnoses on the basis of symptoms.

Equally important, the practice has changed and developed over the centuries. 'Observation as both word and practice wandered from rustic and monastic settings to learned publications' from astronomy in the fifteenth century to medicine in the sixteenth. Observation in the sense of 'a methodical and empirical approach' and 'adherence to detail' became 'part of scientific proof and persuasion'.[8] The seventeenth century, especially in the Netherlands, has been called 'the age of observation'. To be more precise, certain kinds of observation were transformed at this time by the invention of the telescope and the microscope. At about the same time, a number of writers, including physicians, claimed to be able to read hearts and minds by observing the changing expressions of the face. In the eighteenth century, more emphasis was placed on clinical observation in medicine. A Dutch learned society (in Haarlem) offered a prize for an essay on the art of observation (1770), while a 'Société des Observateurs de l'Homme' was founded in France (1790).

In the nineteenth century, when books on 'how to observe' and 'what to observe' appeared in print, the famous study of war by Karl von Clausewitz emphasized the importance of military observation, while the historian August von Schlözer discussed what he called 'the statistical gaze', by which he did not mean looking at figures but the close observation of states by students of politics. Systematic investigations of social conditions on behalf of the government, including the collection of statistics in the modern sense of the term, formed part of what has been described as the 'nineteenth-century revolution in government', dependent on a multitude of 'experts' – inspectors, medical officers, imperial administrators, statisticians and other 'agents of knowledge', together with social surveys that provided information about poverty, literacy, disease and so on.[9] The census is an ancient institution, from China to Israel, but regular censuses of the population of different states only became common practice in the nineteenth century.

A specialized form of observation developed at the turn of the nineteenth and twentieth centuries in order to combat crime, although some of the techniques involved had a wider application. As Carlo Ginzburg noted in the 1970s, the fictional investigator Sherlock Holmes, who claimed that 'there is nothing so important as trifles', was a contemporary of Sigmund Freud, who revealed the significance of small slips of the tongue, and of the scholar-physician Giovanni Morelli, who developed a method for attributing paintings to particular artists by examining with care small details such as the forms of drapery or the shapes of human ears, which each painter – whether consciously or unconsciously – represents in a distinctive manner.[10]

Edmond Locard, sometimes described as the 'Sherlock Holmes of France', opened the first forensic laboratory in Lyon in 1910. Locard became famous for his discussion of the silent testimony of the traces left by human activity on material culture. According to his 'exchange principle', the criminal will bring something to the scene of the crime, if only a few dropped hairs on a carpet, and leave with something from it, thus offering detectives clues linking an individual, a scene and an event. Today's crime scene investigators make use of a sophisticated technology that was unavailable in Locard's time, but they follow in his footsteps.

A relatively new form of observation has come to be practised by anthropologists and sociologists. The phrase 'participant observation' dates from the 1920s and originally referred to a situation where the observer was a member of the group observed, recruited by an outside investigator. Today, on the other hand, it refers to outsiders who join the group they wish to study while remaining as unobtrusive as possible in the circumstances.[11] A still more recent form of observation that spread in both the UK and the USA in the 1980s makes use of closed-circuit television cameras, a visible sign of the 'surveillance society'.

Sending expeditions

Expeditions in search of knowledge, often funded by governments, go back at least as far as the fifteenth century, when the Spanish monarchs Ferdinand and Isabella supported the attempt by Columbus to find a new route to the Indies, accidentally discovering America on the way. In 1570, the government of Philip II of Spain sent the physician Francisco Hernández to Mexico and Central America to discover new plants with medical uses. It was from the eighteenth century onwards, however, that scientific expeditions to different parts of the globe became frequent, sent for the most part by imperial governments – British, French, Spanish, Portuguese, Russian and so on.[12] Astronomers, botanists, naturalists and mineralogists took part in these expeditions, along with artists. For the savants, the purpose of these expeditions was to acquire knowledge for its own sake, while for the organizers, often governments, they formed part of the enterprise of empire. Many specimens were collected; 16,000 plants and seeds were taken to the Royal Botanic Garden in Spain after the Malaspina expedition to the Pacific (1790), while 50,000 specimens were sent back from Rio by the US Exploring Expedition (1838), officially described as undertaken 'to extend the bounds of science and promote the acquisition of knowledge'.

As a case-study of this trend to the collective gathering of knowledge, we might take Captain Cook's first voyage to the Pacific (1768–71), visiting Brazil, Tahiti, New Zealand and Australia. His mission was undertaken at the request of the Royal Society in order to observe the transit of Venus over the sun, a movement that would allow the distance of the earth from the sun to be calculated. Hence Cook was accompanied by the assistant to the Astronomer Royal. Again at the request of the Royal Society, Joseph Banks, a young gentleman amateur with botanical training (not yet the middle-aged knowledge manager whom we met in the previous chapter), was allowed to join the expedition together with his assistants, including two naturalists (one of them the Swede Daniel Solander, who had been trained by the famous Linnaeus) to collect specimens of plants and animals and two artists to record landscapes and peoples encountered during the voyage.

The expedition was supported not only by the Royal Society but also by the Admiralty, which was more concerned with knowledge that might be useful in imperial projects than with pure science. Cook was ordered by the Admiralty to search for undiscovered territories that Britain might claim and to that end he mapped the coast of New Zealand and part of Australia. His instructions, formulated with precision, commanded him 'carefully to observe the Nature of the Soil and the Products thereof; the Beasts and Fowls that inhabit or frequent it; the fishes that are to be found in the Rivers or upon the Coast and in what Plenty; and in case you find any Mines, Minerals or valuable stones, you are to bring home Specimens of each, as also such Specimens of the Seeds of Trees, Fruits and Grains as you may be able to collect'.[13]

The observations made of the transit of Venus did not tell a clear story. However, the expedition did bring back answers to some of the questions formulated in Cook's instructions. Among the 'Beasts', they sighted a kangaroo. They discovered many new plants on the coast of Australia (justifying the name 'Botany Bay') including a spiky flower that is now known as Banksia. Banks extended his interests beyond botany to include the 'manners and customs' of the different peoples encountered on the voyage. It has been noted that his vision of the Pacific was no innocent eye but 'coloured' by his classical education. For example, he saw Tahiti as 'the truest picture of an arcadia'.[14] All the same, Banks's interest in learning something of local languages, notably Tahitian, and his careful observation of costume, ceremonies and customs such as cannibalism and tattooing is worthy of note.[15] In New Zealand, he even insisted on buying and taking home the head of an enemy recently killed by one of the Maori whom the expedition encountered.[16]

Storing and preserving

To be of any use, the information that is gathered needs to be stored and preserved, most obviously by being written down. In the case of the scientific expeditions just mentioned, as in that of individual anthropologists or ethologists, taking 'field-notes' was an important part of their task. In the case of censuses and other social surveys, the information collected ended up in registers, files or in more recent times in databases.

As these stores of knowledge multiplied, keeping them safe became a problem to which the archive offered a solution. In early modern Europe, officials often worked at home and as a consequence treated government papers as their private property, inaccessible to their successors. From the point of view of efficient administration, this was a major inconvenience. As Queen Elizabeth wrote to the Master of the Rolls in 1567, 'It is not meet that the records of our Chancery ... should remain in private places and houses.' Hence governments, following the lead of the Papacy and the Republic of Venice, began to establish archives, complete with keepers and rules governing access. In the nineteenth century, archives gradually opened to the public, 'archivist' became a profession, and some archivists insisted on saving documents that governments wished to destroy, as Francis Palgrave, the first head of the English Public Record Office did in the case of the census returns of 1851. It is only recently, however, that historians, especially historians of knowledge, have come to view archives as an important object of research in themselves as well as a collection of sources for the study of other aspects of the past, so that books and articles on the topic are beginning to proliferate.[17]

When books were relatively few, as in early medieval Europe, copying manuscripts was an important activity and the libraries of leading monasteries were major sites of knowledge. As books multiplied in the late Middle Ages – and still more after the invention of printing – their storage became an increasingly acute problem. The Vatican Library, one of the most important in Europe at this time, consisted of 2,500 volumes in 1475. In 1600 the imperial library in Vienna included 10,000 volumes, but by 1738, the number had increased to 200,000. The library of the British Museum reached 540,000 volumes by 1856. Today, the Library of Congress contains the mind-boggling number of some 100 million items.[18] It is necessary to refer to 'items' rather than to books because today's libraries store information in the form of tapes, CDs, videos and so on. So do governments. Photos were used by the Paris police from 1872 onwards to identify criminals, while the Watergate scandal of the 1970s is a reminder of the importance, to governments and investigative journalists alike, of tape-recorded conversations.

All these items take up space and one of the main problems for modern archivists and librarians has been finding room for the endless flow of new 'acquisitions'. The Italian state archives contained 163,932.57 square metres of shelving in 1906, for instance, while the FBI had accumulated over 65 million cards in its files by 1981. It might be said that the digital revolution came in the nick of time, moving information from the earth to the cloud. By the year 2003, the FBI had a billion files online.

The complementary opposite of preserving knowledge is of course losing it. These losses have a history, including famous events such as the burning of the great library of Alexandria. To loss by accident must be added knowledge that is discarded, books and manuscripts that librarians and archivists 'de-accession', in other words throw away. It was in response to the Italian government's plan to discard most of the files from the census of 1928 that the famous statistician Corrado Gini developed a method of sampling. On a grander scale, whole fields of knowledge, from alchemy to phrenology to eugenics, have lost their respectability and virtually disappeared from the academic world, even if they sometimes survive on its margins.[19]

Retrieving

Today, databases are organized for rapid retrieval, complementing or replacing earlier systems. Human memory is obviously the oldest form of retrieval, sometimes assisted by training in the 'art of memory', which in the ancient world and again in the Renaissance involved associating what needed to be remembered with vivid images arranged in an imaginary building such as a memory palace or theatre.[20] Memory might be assisted by objects such as the knotted and coloured cords used in Peru under the Incas and known as *qipus*.

For archivists and librarians, organizing their material in order to facilitate retrieval is an old problem. In large early modern archives such as that of the Venetian government, there was not only a catalogue but also indexes of names and subjects, while other archivists preferred to arrange material in chronological order. In the nineteenth century, a new principle for organizing archives was formulated, the principle of provenance. That is, documents came to be arranged according to the institution that created them, making it easier for researchers to imagine past administrators at work.

Librarians faced similar problems to archivists. In the case of small libraries, consisting of no more than a few hundred books, the solution was simple: to compile a catalogue informing readers on which shelf a given manuscript was to be found. The larger the library, however, the larger the problem. In the most famous library of the ancient world, the library of Alexandria, founded in the third century BCE, the collection consisted of scrolls, so that viewing the contents took much longer than opening a modern book. Searching half a million scrolls was a serious problem, even if it was alleviated by tags attached to the edge of the scroll, by labels on the bins in which the scroll was stored and by an innovation that would turn into a tradition, a catalogue of authors and subjects. These catalogues were first written on scrolls, then in bound volumes and finally on cards arranged in drawers. It was the American librarian Melvil Dewey who standardized the size of the cards, at 125×75 millimetres, and formed a company, the Library Bureau, to sell the cards and other equipment such as the filing cabinets that housed them. Scholars too found cards a convenient means of arranging their notes, replacing the more fragile slips of paper they had used in the seventeenth and eighteenth centuries. Even in the digital age, some scholars still make notes in this way.

The subject catalogue was a solution to a problem that raised problems of its own. Paraphrasing Plato, one might say that, in the ideal library, the librarian should be a philosopher or a philosopher should become the librarian. In fact, this combination famously occurred at the library of Wolfenbüttel in Germany, where Gottfried Wilhelm Leibniz worked from 1691 to his death in 1716. Leibniz combined a philosopher's interest in the organization of knowledge with a librarian's interest in classifying books. He preferred a practical to a logical classification, remarking that 'those who arrange a library very often do not know where to place certain books, being in suspense between two or three places equally suitable'. In all his years as librarian, he was happy to accept the traditional classification of books according to academic disciplines – arts, medicine, law and theology – while introducing new categories where necessary, among them for books on craft skills, located under *mechanica* and *oeconomica*.[21]

The most famous system for classifying books was developed by Melvil Dewey. It was the so-called DDC or Dewey Decimal Classification, first published in 1876 and gradually expanded and improved in successive editions – eighteen in all. It has been adopted by many libraries in many parts of the world. It also inspired the Belgian Paul Otlet in his attempt to organize knowledge in general, to 'catalogue the world' in the service of world peace and, he hoped, world government (active in the first half of the twentieth century, Otlet was a warm supporter of the League of Nations). An enthusiast for new technology, in his case microfilm and the telegraph, Otlet dreamt of freeing the organization of knowledge from the organization of books, planning a collection of images and a sound archive and imagining, in the 1930s, a 'world network' of information not far removed in conception from today's Internet.[22]

The proliferation of books posed problems for readers as well as librarians. It has been said that 'the half of knowledge is knowing where to find it'. As Samuel Johnson remarked to his friend Boswell, 'Knowledge is of two kinds. We know a subject ourselves, or we know where we can find information upon it. When we enquire into any subject, the first thing we have to do is to know what books have treated of it. This leads us to look at catalogues, and at the backs of books in libraries.' In this case too, procedures have changed over time. From the early seventeenth century onwards, printed subject bibliographies helped to orient would-be readers. They multiplied so fast that as early as 1664 one scholar thought it necessary to produce a bibliography of bibliographies. In similar fashion, a dictionary of dictionaries (including encyclopaedias) was published in 1758.

Finding the right book was not enough. There remained the problem of finding information in it. Hence the gradual rise, after Gutenberg, of finding devices such as tables of contents, indexes, or summaries of chapters or paragraphs printed in the margin of the book. As tables, charts and graphs became more common, there emerged the problem of learning to read them, sometimes described as 'consultation literacy'.

For individuals needing information on particular subjects in a hurry, the encyclopaedia – large or small, general or specialized – has long offered a solution to their problems, not only in the West but in the Islamic and East Asian worlds as well. The Chinese encyclopaedic tradition goes back to the third century CE, while Chinese encyclopaedias reached vast dimensions long before Western ones. The early fifteenth-century *Great Handbook* (*Yongle dadian*) involved some two thousand contributors and ran to more than ten thousand volumes, making it too expensive to print, while the *Collection of Pictures and Writings* (*Tushu Jicheng*), contained more than three-quarters of a million pages, making it in all probability the longest printed book in the world.

How to organize this mass of information posed a problem for the Chinese, just as it did for the editors of the great French *Encyclopédie* (1751–65) or the *Encyclopaedia*

Britannica (first edition, 1768–71). The traditional method of organization for Western encyclopaedias, as for library catalogues, was by subject, following the university curriculum. However, the editors of the *Encyclopédie*, with some regret, opted for what they called the 'dictionary principle', in other words, entries arranged in alphabetical order. This solution was of course unavailable to the Chinese, who do not use an alphabet. Their traditional arrangement distinguished three large categories (heaven, earth and humanity) with many sub-divisions.

In the last few decades, encyclopaedias have gone online, the *Britannica* (1994) no less than *Wikipedia* (2001), forming part of a major shift in the way in which many people seek information, a shift that has prompted one writer to claim that we now live in 'Search Engine Society'. Searching online, like searching in libraries, requires particular skills. What has been described as 'search engine literacy' is replacing older forms of consultation literacy. It includes not only the formulation of fruitful questions but also an awareness of the built-in biases of the engines, which are of course driven by advertising.[23]

Analysing Knowledges

It is time to move from retrieval to analysis. 'Analysis' is a technical term with rather different meanings in different disciplines: algebraic analysis, analytical chemistry, analytical philosophy, spectroscopic analysis, tissue analysis, psychoanalysis and so on. In chemistry, for instance, analysis involves breaking down substances into their constituents. By contrast, historical analysis depends on synthesis, the combination of pieces of information like fragments of a jigsaw puzzle in order to construct explanations of events and trends. In sociology and anthropology, 'functional analysis', an approach that was widespread in the mid twentieth century, meant – like psychoanalysis – rejecting the explanations of actions given by the actors themselves and offering new explanations that claimed to be more profound.

In what follows, however, the term 'analysis' will be used to refer to what I described earlier as 'cooking', in other words the process of turning information into knowledge by means of practices such as description, quantification, classification and verification. They too have their history. The seventeenth century, for instance, was the heyday of the so-called 'geometrical method', applied to subjects ranging from physics to ethics, politics and even history. Thomas Hobbes's *Leviathan* (1651) showed that its author was, as his friend John Aubrey described him, 'in love with geometry'. Spinoza described his *Ethics* (1677) as 'proved geometrically' (*ordine geometrico demonstrata*), listing axioms and deducing conclusions. In a treatise published in 1679, a French bishop, Pierre-Daniel Huet, tried to establish the truth of Christianity on the basis of 'axioms' such as the following: 'Every historical work is truthful, if it tells what happened in the way in which it is told in many books which are contemporary or more or less contemporary to the events narrated.' A Scottish theologian, John Craig, both an acquaintance and a follower of Isaac Newton, formulated what he called the *Rules of Historical Evidence* (1699) in the form of axioms and theorems. Unfortunately these axioms and theorems, like Huet's, turned out to be rather banal, using the language of mathematics and physics to restate commonplaces, for example the principle that the reliability of sources varies according to the distance of the witness from the event recorded.

Description

Description is often contrasted with analysis but the careful description of what has been observed is an indispensable stage in the analytic process. Like observation, description is a practice that might appear to be timeless – yet it has a history, becoming increasingly precise, systematic and specialized. In the West, for example, the tradition of describing places goes back to the ancient Greeks, notably to Strabo, while the precise description of plants and animals goes back to the Renaissance. The description of plants in particular became more detailed, more precise and more methodical, more concerned with the differences between one species of plant and others, hence more and more reliant on illustrations to complement the information conveyed in words.[24] It has been argued that seventeenth-century Dutch art was an 'art of describing', as opposed to the narrative art of the Italians, and that it was linked both to map-making, an art that the Dutch dominated at this time, and to observation through the microscope, a Dutch invention of the same period.[25] In similar fashion, some English artists have been described as careful observers of either nature or society; Hogarth, for instance, with his sharp eye for the details of manners and customs, or Constable, with his attention to the precise forms of trees or clouds.[26]

Early modern antiquarians, in other words scholars who studied the material remains of the past, offered increasingly precise descriptions of their finds, together with illustrations, as the eighteenth-century English scholar William Stukeley did in the case of Stonehenge. From the late eighteenth century, the police in France and elsewhere became concerned with the precise description of wanted criminals. Like botanists, they turned to drawings (and later, to photographs) to help them in their task. Early modern Venetian ambassadors were required to produce a 'report' (*relazione*) on their return, analysing the strengths and weaknesses of the state in which they had been residing. From the eighteenth century onwards, the many scientific expeditions undertaken also produced masses of reports, describing what had been discovered. In the nineteenth century, the practice of reporting spread more and more widely together with the apparatus of bureaucracy. A series of reports by committees, the prologue to government action, were published in nineteenth-century England: the Sadler Report (1832) on the conditions of child labour and female labour in factories, for instance, the Report of Commissioners Appointed to Inquire into the British Museum (1850) or the Northcote-Trevelyan Report (1854) on the reform of the civil service.

As we have seen, some nineteenth-century scholars looked down on what they called 'mere' description, as practised by the naturalists, for instance. In response, two defences of description were formulated. One defence, linking description to interpretation, will be discussed later in this chapter. The other was to make description more precise by means of quantification.

Quantification

In order to be precise, descriptions needed to include measurements and other numbers. Some eighteenth-century scientists measured and even weighed the earth. In the nineteenth century, chemists undertook quantitative analysis of different substances to discover the relative importance of their constituents, physicists measured changes in matter and energy and astronomers collected stellar statistics. Alexander von Humboldt became famous for his contribution to different sciences, from botanical geography to geophysics, by means of quantitative methods and a whole arsenal of scientific instruments. Francis Galton played an important part in the development of biostatistics.

Social surveys increasingly included tables of figures, so that the term 'statistics' acquired a new meaning as a synonym for what used to be known as 'political arithmetic'. In the late eighteenth century the French government, assisted by leading mathematicians such as Condorcet, became a pioneer in collecting and analysing statistics.[27] New methods of visual display such as the graph and the 'pie chart' developed in order to communicate the results of measurement more rapidly and more memorably. In late eighteenth-century Britain, William Playfair, an engineer turned economist, was a pioneer in this domain.[28] By the later nineteenth century, statistical offices formed part of the administration in a number of countries in Europe. Scholars in the social sciences followed this lead; economists measuring 'gross natural product', for instance, students of elections (sometimes described as 'psephologists') counting votes and sociologists analysing statistics in order to discover the relation between trends in crime, education, health and so on. Anthropologists turned to 'anthropometry', measuring bodies, especially skulls, in order to identify different peoples, a technique borrowed by the French police officer Alphonse Bertillon (the son of a statistician) to identify individuals by their physical measurements.

In the humanities, by contrast, quantitative methods were slower to come into use and their relevance remains controversial. In the case of texts, quantitative content analysis (counting the frequency of certain words, for instance) has often been used to identify the authorship of anonymous works. As for history, by the middle of the twentieth century, a substantial group of economic, social and political historians were employing quantitative methods, mockingly described by opponents of the trend as 'cliometrics', the vital statistics of the goddess of history.

Classifying knowledges

Precise description assisted the process of classification, as in the well-known case of the eighteenth-century Swedish scholar Carl Linnaeus, whose ambitions were summed up in the title of his most famous work, 'The system of nature' (*Systema Naturae*, 1735). His famous binomial scheme for classifying plants, giving each one two names, one for the genus or family and the other for the individual species, was published in 1753. Although the system of Linnaeus was controversial, and abandoned by nineteenth-century botanists in favour of a more 'natural' system, his method remained an inspiration to scholars working in other disciplines and attempting to classify animals, diseases, minerals, chemical compounds and even clouds. Linguists too engaged in classification, arranging related languages into families such as 'Indo-European' or 'Ural-Altaic'.

Debates about classification in particular disciplines were extended, almost inevitably, to knowledge itself, often imagined as a tree with many branches. The traditional Western system, following the university curriculum, distinguished theology, law and medicine (the three subjects of postgraduate studies in the Middle Ages), from 'arts'. In its turn arts, otherwise known as the 'liberal arts', distinguished the more elementary *trivium*, a package of grammar, logic and rhetoric, from the more advanced *quadrivium*, comprising arithmetic, geometry, astronomy and music. The degree of BA, 'bachelor of arts', originally referred to these seven liberal arts. The non-academic knowledges that remained were described in parallel fashion as the seven 'mechanical arts'. There was some disagreement about the contents of this package, but weaving, agriculture, architecture, metallurgy, trade, cooking, navigation and warfare frequently recur.

Over the centuries many suggestions were put forward for reorganizing the system. Renaissance humanists, for instance, following the example of ancient Rome, stressed what they called the *studia humanitatis*: grammar, rhetoric, poetry, history and ethics. It is from these studies that the words 'humanist' and 'humanities' are derived. Francis Bacon advocated a division of knowledges into three major sections, each associated with one of the three 'faculties' of the human mind: memory (including history), reason (including mathematics and law) and imagination (including art). Bacon's system was accepted, with modifications, by the editors of the French *Encyclopédie*, even though they decided to arrange their articles in alphabetical order. Indirectly, Bacon inspired Melvil Dewey's Decimal Classification System, still in use in many of the world's libraries.

There is no equivalent to the Decimal Classification System for use in museums, where the arrangement of objects has sometimes been controversial. In the 1890s, for instance, the anthropologist Franz Boas caused a sensation in the American museum world by criticizing the organization of exhibits in the Smithsonian Institution. The exhibits were arranged in the way customary at that time, according to the assumption of what Boas called 'a uniform systematic history of the evolution of culture'. What he preferred was what he called 'tribal arrangement of collections' in what would become known as 'culture areas'. The North West Coast Hall, which Boas arranged in the Museum of Natural History in New York, illustrates his approach and his view of objects as so many witnesses to the nature of the culture in which they were produced. Exhibits, he argued, could 'show how far each and every civilization is the outcome of its geography and historical surroundings'. Indeed, an object, according to Boas, could not be understood 'outside of its surroundings' (or, as we often say today, its context).

To illustrate this point, Boas took the example of a pipe. 'A pipe of the North American Indians', he argued, 'is not only a curious implement out of which the Indian smokes, but it has a great number of uses and meanings, which can be understood only when viewed from the standpoint of the social and religious life of the people.' Hence Boas liked to show 'life groups' in the museum, with waxworks of people in the act of using the objects, in order 'to transport the visitor into foreign surroundings' and to allow an appreciation of an alien culture as a whole.[29]

Comparing

Classification depended on comparison and contrast. The comparative method became increasingly important in the academic world of the mid nineteenth century. One of its great successes was comparative anatomy, in other words the study of both similarities and differences in the anatomy of different species. Already in the sixteenth century, some scholars had compared and contrasted the skeletons of humans with those of animals, but it was Georges Cuvier who employed the comparative method in *Leçons d'anatomie comparée* (1800) and other works to reconstruct extinct species of animal, such as the dinosaurs, on the basis of the fragmentary evidence of fossils.

Philology was another field where the systematic use of the comparative method led to new discoveries, such as the descent of Greek and Latin from Sanskrit, discovered by the lawyer William Jones ('Oriental Jones') when he was living in Calcutta, or the structural similarities between languages with very different vocabularies, such as Hungarian and Finnish. A major work in this field was the *Vergleichende Grammatik* ('Comparative Grammar'), published from 1833 onwards by Franz Bopp, a professor of Sanskrit who extended his interests to what he called the 'Indo-European' languages.

The comparison of languages stimulated the comparison of religions and mythologies. Jones noted similarities between the Hindu gods and those of the Greeks and Romans. The German philologist Max Müller, a specialist on Sanskrit, published a study of comparative mythology in 1856 and became professor of comparative theology in Oxford in 1868 (the new field became better known as 'comparative religion'). A century after Müller, the French scholar Georges Dumézil spent much of his career studying similarities between Indian, Greek, Roman, Norse and Celtic mythologies, all from parts of the world where 'Indo-European' languages were spoken. He replaced the earlier concern with similar gods, such as Jupiter and Odin, with a concern with system, which he called 'ideology', emphasizing the relation of different gods to praying, fighting and farming, the 'three functions' that underlie many social structures.[30]

The comparative method was used not only to establish genealogies of languages, gods or myths but also to assist explanation. As we have seen, Herbert Spencer wished to establish a new discipline under the title of 'comparative sociology'. Some historians, not content simply to supply the raw material for sociologists to construct their theories, wrote comparative studies such as the 'parallel' between the histories of Spain and Poland published by the Polish historian Joachim Lelewel in 1831. In his *System of Logic* (1843), the philosopher John Stuart Mill reflected on the use of comparison in the search for causes, emphasizing the importance of what he called 'concomitant variation', in other words what is now known as the 'correlation' between two sets of data.

Interpretation

It is obviously difficult to distinguish interpretation from description and even from observation. All the same, it is possible to distinguish an interpretive method, or cluster of methods. Where comparison, like the functional analysis that used to be practised in sociology and anthropology, offers a view from outside, the interpretive method, which is common to a number of disciplines, attempts understanding from within. The method, which is thousands of years old and can be found in different cultures, was elaborated and systematized in the study of texts, religious texts such as the Bible and the Koran and secular texts such as Roman law. In Renaissance Europe, one school of lawyers, following what was known as the 'French style' (*mos gallicus*), interpreted laws in an historical manner by examining the way in which the main concepts were used and attempting to reconstruct the intentions of the legislators and the circumstances, or, as we now say, the cultural 'context', in which the laws were formulated. The idea of context itself has a history.[31]

Adopting a similar approach to the Bible was more risky, in both the Catholic and Protestant worlds, but the tendency to interpret the Bible as an historical document, or more exactly an anthology of historical documents, gradually became more powerful in the eighteenth and nineteenth centuries. The parallels between the problems of interpreting the Bible and interpreting texts from ancient Greece and Rome caught the attention of a number of scholars (notably the German theologian Friedrich Schleiermacher) and led to the development of 'hermeneutics'. This was a general method of approaching texts that emphasized the value of the 'hermeneutic circle', interpreting the parts with reference to the whole and the whole with reference to the parts. At the end of the nineteenth century, Sigmund Freud extended the approach to the unconscious mind in his famous *Traumdeutung* ('Interpretation of Dreams', 1899). Systematic attempts to interpret dreams go back to ancient Greece or beyond, but Freud tried to place these approaches to dreams on a new basis.

In the twentieth century, interpretation was extended still further, illustrating once again the transfer or translation of a method from one discipline to others. Art historians began to practice the interpretation of images at two levels, not only 'iconography' (concerned with the manifest content of an image) but also what a leading practitioner of the method, Erwin Panofsky, called 'iconology' (examining its deeper cultural significance).[32] More recently, some musicologists have described themselves as doing 'musical hermeneutics', an approach that, 'like psychoanalysis, seeks meaning in places where meaning is often said not to be found'.[33] In archaeology, some British scholars made an 'interpretive turn' and described themselves as 'reading' artefacts in order to reconstruct past meanings. Whether the participants realized this, their movement, also known as 'contextual archaeology', followed a German hermeneutical tradition, although it was actually inspired by the British philosopher-historian R. G. Collingwood and the American anthropologist Clifford Geertz.[34] Rejecting the mode of analysis from outside that is characteristic of the natural sciences, Geertz and his followers turned to the interpretation of human behaviour, treating different cultures as texts that needed to be 'read'. The practitioners of interpretive anthropology described their own work as 'thick description', a form of description that, like iconology, included interpretation. In this way they responded both to the depreciation of 'mere' description and to the emphasis on functional analysis in the work of their colleagues.[35] Retrospectively, one might extend the idea of thick description to include two historical masterpieces, Jacob Burckhardt's *Cultur der Renaissance in Italien* ('Civilization of the Renaissance in Italy', 1860) and Johan Huizinga's *Herfstij der Middeleeuwen* ('Autumn of the Middle Ages', 1919).

Verification

How do we know that our knowledge is reliable? What counts as proof, or as evidence? Each discipline has to face the problem of verification. Like observation and description, methods of verification have a history, the study of which is known as 'historical epistemology', concerned with changes in the justifications for belief and in the methods of acquiring knowledge. A pioneer in this field was the historian of philosophy Ernst Cassirer, whose study of the problem of knowledge in early modern Europe was published in 1906–7. In the preface to this work, Cassirer criticized the assumption that the 'instruments of thought' (by which he meant fundamental concepts) are timeless. On the contrary, he argued, each epoch has its own. Recent scholars have gone further in this direction, expanding the idea of 'instruments of thought' to include scientific instruments such as telescopes, which have become larger, more sophisticated and more powerful over the centuries.[36]

A vivid example of past practice, reminding us that 'the past is a foreign country', comes from Steven Shapin's provocatively entitled *Social History of Truth*, in which he argued that trust in the word of a gentleman in seventeenth-century England extended to accounts of experiments conducted and witnessed by natural philosophers.[37] On the other hand, the increasing importance of systematically repeated experiments as a confirmation of scientific discoveries offers a famous example of change in methods of verification. It has been argued that this trend exemplifies 'the rise of the methods of the manual workers to the ranks of academically trained scholars at the end of the sixteenth century'.[38] Beginning in physics and chemistry, experimental methods were gradually extended to new fields such as medicine, agriculture, biology and psychology.

The rise of the practice of 'experiment', a term related to 'experience', was part of a wider change that might be described as the increasing importance of empiricism in the academic world. Academics who claimed to be masters of *scientia* used to look down on mere 'empirics' such as the healers or artisans who practised on the basis of experience alone. Francis Bacon, however, argued for the value of a middle way. 'Those who have handled sciences', he wrote, 'have been either men of experiment or men of dogmas. The men of experiment are like the ant, they only collect and use; the reasoners resemble spiders, who make cobwebs out of their own substance. But the bee takes a middle course: it gathers its material from the flowers of the garden and of the field, but transforms and digests it by a power of its own.'

Another example of change in methods of proof is the medical autopsy, in other words the examination and where necessary the dissection of corpses to determine the cause of death, thus verifying earlier diagnoses that depended on the evidence of symptoms. Autopsy has a long history – it was practised in ancient Egypt – but its place in medicine became increasingly important in the eighteenth century. A third example of major change concerns the law.[39] In Europe in the Middle Ages, for instance, in cases of dispute, the old way for courts to discover what had happened was to ask witnesses, usually older local men of good standing and long memories. The new way, competing with the old, was to make use of the evidence of written documents (the word 'evidence', which originally meant whatever was clear or conspicuous, extended its meaning in fifteenth-century England to include documents that could be produced in court).[40]

It took time for people to learn to trust writing. In a dispute between King Henry I and the Archbishop of

Canterbury in the early twelfth century, the king's supporters described a letter from the Pope in support of the archbishop as 'only a sheepskin marked with black ink', unworthy of comparison with 'the assertions of three bishops'. In similar fashion an eleventh-century Muslim traveller, al-Beruni, quoted Socrates to the effect that he did not write books because 'I do not transplant knowledge from the living hearts of human beings to the dead skins of sheep.' All the same, the value of oral testimony in different contexts was increasingly devalued from the seventeenth century onwards. The upper and middle classes came to associate it with the ignorance of their social inferiors, while the eighteenth-century scholar William Robertson, in his *History of America*, assumed its untrustworthiness: 'the memory of past transactions can neither be long preserved, nor be transmitted with any fidelity by tradition'.[41] It was only very slowly that belief in the value of oral tradition revived, among nineteenth-century folklorists, for instance, or twentieth century oral historians, and then only on condition that it was studied critically.

Another major change in the practice of the courts was the shift from the language of proof to the language of probability. Some sixteenth-century Italian lawyers already distinguished between 'full' and 'partial' proof, but it was only gradually that lawyers developed a set of concepts to describe the partial or weaker forms: 'presumptive proof', for instance, 'moral certainty', 'circumstantial evidence', 'probable cause' or 'beyond reasonable doubt'. When mathematicians and philosophers began to investigate probability in the seventeenth century, they borrowed ideas from the lawyers. John Locke included an important discussion of 'degrees' of probable knowledge in the fourth part of his essay *Concerning Human Understanding* (1690). In their turn, lawyers made use of Locke's ideas, among them the judge Jeffrey Gilbert, whose *Law of Evidence* was published in 1754.[42]

The methods for identifying the individuals responsible for crimes, especially murder, became more systematic in the nineteenth and twentieth centuries with the rise of police forces and professional detectives. Quintilian, an ancient Roman writer on rhetoric, had already noted the importance of bloodstains as a sign of murder, and 'signs' (*indicia*) of this kind were also discussed by early modern lawyers, but the methodical study of what became known in English as 'clues' came much later, forming part of what became known as 'forensic science'.

The legal model of witnesses and testimonies spread to other disciplines. Experiments, for instance, were described in the language of trials. Again, take the case of what is known as 'textual criticism', the attempt to reconstruct the original version of a given text. The different manuscript versions of parts of the Bible or printed versions of plays by Shakespeare have often been described as 'witnesses', more or less reliable.[43] In the Islamic world, establishing the reliability of the *hadith* (reports of the sayings of Muhammad) depends on the *isnad*, the chain of witnesses leading back to the person who originally heard a given saying.[44]

Again, the early modern Catholic Church instituted more rigorous procedures for canonizing saints, a kind of trial in which the so-called 'devil's advocate' tried to find weaknesses in the evidence for sanctity. In the case of history, the seventeenth-century English lawyer turned historian, John Selden, described the process of evaluating historical sources as 'a kind of trial'. In the twentieth century, following the rise of the detective novel, leading British historians such as R. G. Collingwood and Herbert Butterfield described members of their profession as detectives, following clues in order to establish the facts of the case.

Discovering facts

The idea of 'the facts', distinguished from gossip, conjecture and other forms of unreliable discourse, is central to empiricism in general and to history in particular. It too derives from the courts, which from ancient Rome onwards distinguished matters of fact from matters of law. Francis Bacon, a lawyer turned historian, declared that 'The Register of Knowledge of Fact is called History.' Bacon was also a pioneer in extending the use of the term 'fact' to natural phenomena, which he described as 'the deeds and works of nature', deeds that needed to be verified by observation and experiment. In similar fashion, the history of the Royal

Society by Thomas Sprat described its members as concerned with 'matters of fact'.[45] Seventeenth-century English historians used the language of fact when they claimed to offer an 'impartial' view of conflicts. In 1652, Oliver Cromwell asked the scholar Meric Casaubon to write a history of the Civil War with 'nothing but matters of fact, according to most impartial accounts on both sides', while after the Restoration, Nathaniel Crouch claimed to present an 'Impartial Account' of Cromwell, 'Relating only matters of Fact'.

As in the case of 'evidence', so in that of 'fact' we find that a term in legal discourse gradually spread much more widely. Emile Durkheim defined sociology as 'the science of social facts' (*la science des faits sociaux*), while his follower Marcel Mauss introduced the idea of the 'total social fact' (*fait social total*).[46] On the other hand, scholars who emphasized facts were mocked by colleagues who stressed interpretation as 'fact-worshippers'.

Criticizing history: sceptics and sources

As a case-study in the problems of verification we might turn to the history of history itself, focusing on Europe in the seventeenth and eighteenth centuries, when some scholars, known at the time as 'pyrrhonists' (after the ancient Greek sceptic Pyrrho of Elis), claimed that much that passed for historical knowledge was not knowledge at all. The problem was the failure of historical knowledge to measure up to strict standards of certainty, notably the epistemological standards formulated by René Descartes. This problem was made more acute by the intellectual wars between Catholics and Protestants, in which both sides were more successful in undermining the authority to which the other side appealed (tradition on one side, the Bible on the other) than in supporting their own. It has also been suggested that scepticism was encouraged – indeed popularized – in seventeenth- and eighteenth-century Europe as an unintended consequence of the rise of a new literary genre, the newspaper, since different papers offered conflicting accounts of the same event.[47]

The sceptics employed two main arguments. In the first place, they emphasized the problem of bias, contrasting

Catholic and Protestant accounts of the Reformation or the narratives of battles and wars produced by the two opposing sides, such as France and Spain. They also accused earlier scholars of basing their accounts of the past on forged documents and of writing about characters who had never existed and events that had never taken place. 'Did Romulus exist?' they asked. 'Did Aeneas ever go to Italy?' 'Did the Trojan War take place, or was it just the subject of Homer's "romance"'?

The defenders of historical practice responded to both arguments. In the first place, they suggested that historians could be impartial and simply tell the story of what happened. Ranke's famous formula, 'what actually happened', was anticipated by an eighteenth-century German historian who declared that the historian 'must present a fact just as it happened' (*Er muss die Sache so vorstellen, wie sie Geschehen ist*). The defence sometimes claimed certainty, but they were usually content to admit that their conclusions about what happened in the past were no more than probable.

For example, Locke argued in response to the sceptics that some historical statements are more probable than others and that some cannot reasonably be denied. 'When any particular matter of fact is vouched by concurrent testimony of unsuspected witnesses, there our consent is ... unavoidable. Thus: that there is such a city in Italy as Rome; that about 1700 years ago there lived in it a man, called Julius Caesar; that he was a general, and that he won a battle against another, called Pompey.' Friedrich Wilhelm Bierling, a professor at the university of Rinteln in Saxony who published a treatise on scepticism about the past in 1724, followed Locke in distinguishing levels of probability in history, three in all, from the maximum (that Julius Caesar existed), via the middle level (the reasons for the abdication of Charles V) to the minimum (the problem of the complicity of Mary Queen of Scots in the murder of her husband, or of Wallenstein's plans in the months before his assassination).

In the second place, the defence argued that it was possible to examine the 'sources' for history with a critical eye. In 1681, for example, responding to a Jesuit who had questioned the authenticity of royal charters in early medieval France, the Benedictine scholar Jean Mabillon published a treatise discussing the methods of dating such documents by the study of their handwriting, their formulae, their seals, and so on. In this way he showed how forgeries might be detected and the authenticity of other charters vindicated. Hence it might be argued that the negative arguments of the sceptics had a positive effect, to make historians more aware of their methods and more critical of their sources than they had been. They now quoted more documents and offered more references in their footnotes, so that readers could if they wished follow them back to the sources. To do this was to write 'critical history', a scholarly slogan of the early eighteenth century.[48]

Criticism

The term 'critic' has changed its meaning over the centuries. The Latin word *criticus* originally meant a philologist engaged in the activity now known as 'textual criticism', in other words the attempt, mentioned earlier, to establish what an author originally wrote by studying the different manuscripts of a given text, each of them different, since it is impossible to transcribe even a fairly short text without making mistakes. Thanks to principles such as the authority of the earlier manuscript or the more difficult reading, scholarly editors produced emended versions of texts, even though some emendations remained – and still remain – controversial, above all when they concern a sacred text such as the Bible.

Gradually, the practice of textual criticism was extended to the dating of a given text, its authorship (including the detection of forgeries), the sources used by the author and the cultural contexts in which the text was written and transmitted. For example, the Old Testament was the subject of a controversial study by the Catholic scholar Richard Simon, the *Histoire Critique du Vieux Testament* (1678), discussing the history of the transmission of the text and the possible authorship of different parts of it (Simon was one of the scholars who argued against the tradition that Moses had written the first five books of the Bible). In the mid eighteenth century, another French scholar, Jean Astruc, argued that the book of Genesis, which used two different words for God,

Elohim and Yahweh, was based on two earlier texts, now lost. This kind of investigation of the different parts of the Bible became known as the 'higher criticism' (as distinct from 'lower' emendations of the text).

This higher criticism was extended to other texts, notably to Homer's epics the *Iliad* and the *Odyssey*. The Neapolitan historian Giambattista Vico had already argued in his *Scienza Nuova* (1744) that the two epics had been written by different individuals living in different centuries. The German scholar Friedrich Wolf went further in is *Prolegomena ad Homerum* (1795), demonstrating that the Homeric poems were transmitted orally and written down much later. Literary criticism gradually emerged from textual criticism in the nineteenth century, at a time when the methods of textual criticism were extended from classical and biblical studies to medieval and modern vernacular literatures, notably by Karl Lachmann in his editions of medieval German poems.

Literary criticism combined and still combines a number of intellectual genres. These genres include the editing of literary texts; their interpretation (once again adapting methods for interpreting the Bible and classical writers such as Homer and Virgil); the analysis of literary techniques (formerly studied under the rubric 'rhetoric'); the history of literary genres; the biography of authors; and 'literary criticism' in a narrower sense, the evaluation of novels, poems, plays and so on. The approach advocated in an American movement of the 1940s, the 'New Criticism', was a kind of return to philology in the sense of emphasizing the 'close reading' of texts, though at the expense of context. Context had its revenge in the form of a later American movement within literary studies, the 'New Historicism' of the 1980s.

In the case of history, nineteenth-century German scholars developed the method of 'source criticism' (*Quellenkritik*), the systematic evaluation of testimonies about the past by considering whether their authors had first-hand or only second-hand knowledge of the topic they were writing about. In what became a classic study, Barthold Niebuhr, writing what he called 'critical history', rejected the account of the early Roman past given by Livy, who lived centuries later than the events he recounted, and tried to reconstruct the sources that Livy had followed. Inspired by Niebuhr, Leopold von Ranke produced a *Kritik neueren Geschichtschreiber* ('Critique of Modern Historians', 1824). In this essay Ranke analysed, indeed took apart, the famous history of Italy written in the sixteenth century by Francesco Guicciardini, asking 'if his information was original, or if borrowed, in what manner it was borrowed and what kind of research was employed to compile it'. These questions have become routine for historians and they have been extended from texts to images and also to the testimonies collected by oral historians.

Other forms of criticism have less to do with the tradition of studying texts. Immanuel Kant's *Kritik der Reinen Vernunft* ('Critique of Pure Reason', 1781) examined the limitations of human reason. Following Marx's claim that philosophers have only interpreted the world, while 'the point is to change it', the Frankfurt School of philosophers and sociologists offered a critique as well as an analysis of the society that they lived in. Their approach became known as 'critical theory', following the publication of Max Horkheimer's *Traditionelle und Kritische Theorie* ('Traditional and Critical Theory', 1937). It has inspired recent movements in other disciplines such as 'critical ethnography' and 'critical legal studies', concerned to change social and institutional systems as well as to study them.

Narrating

The final stage in the long process of analysis in a number of different fields is to produce a synthesis intended to contribute to knowledge in the sense of understanding. These syntheses often take the form of narratives.

Accounts by travellers, including reports on scientific expeditions, are normally arranged in chronological order. Histories too have traditionally been written in a narrative mode, with exceptions such as the famous 'portraits of an age' by Burckhardt and Huizinga, mentioned earlier. Indeed, it has been argued that historical narrative produces knowledge by revealing connections and so making experience comprehensible.[49] In the nineteenth century, a turn to narrative became visible in a number of disciplines, including the

natural sciences. Darwin's *Origin of Species* (1858), an 'evolutionary narrative' that has been compared to Victorian
novels, is simply the most famous example of a scientific
work that took this form.[50] Narratives of experiments, published in specialist journals, remain an important form for
contributions to scientific knowledge.

The major collective exception to the rule that historians
write narratives is the revolt against the history of events
(*histoire événementielle*) mounted by the group of historians
known as the '*Annales* School' from the 1930s onwards,
notably by Fernand Braudel in a study of the Mediterranean
world in the age of Philip II that was published in 1949.
Braudel preferred a descriptive-analytical mode in the first
and second parts of this massive study, concerned respectively with historical geography and social history, although
he did narrate events in the third and final part of his book.
In Britain, R. H. Tawney, a sympathizer with the *Annales*
historians, argued in his inaugural lecture as Professor of
Economic History at the London School of Economics in
1932 that historians should be concerned with society rather
than events, and with analysis rather than narrative. It is of
course no accident that economic historians were prominent
in the revolt against narrative, since many of their analyses
and conclusions did not fit easily into this literary form.

All the same, the philosopher Paul Ricoeur claimed that
even Braudel offered his readers a kind of narrative, since the
three parts of his book were held together by concern with
the long term or *longue durée*. 'To understand this mediation
performed by the long time-span', wrote Ricoeur, is 'to recognize the plot-like character of the whole'.[51] Economic historians who study trends, not to mention major events such
as the Great Crash of 1929, also have more recourse to narrative than Tawney admitted.

By the end of the 1970s, a revival of narrative was under
way among academic historians, fuelled by disillusionment
with economic determinism.[52] However, as is often the case
with revivals, there was no simple return to the past. Suspicion of the oversimplifications of what is often called 'Grand
Narrative', notably 'the rise of the West', together with an
increasing interest in the experiences of ordinary people,
encouraged a number of scholars to write micro-narratives

such as the Italian historian Carlo Ginzburg's *Il formaggio e i vermi* ('Cheese and Worms', 1976) in which the protagonist of the story is a sixteenth-century miller. At more or less the same time, interest in narrative spread among scholars working in other disciplines. For example, an interest in stories on the part of sociologists and anthropologists was associated with increasing respect for the intelligence and the experience of the people they study, who were no longer treated as mere 'objects' of research but as subjects who understood their own culture better than the 'social scientists' who viewed it from outside. Geertz's famous study of the Balinese cockfight, for instance, described it as a text, compared it to plays by Shakespeare and novels by Dostoyevsky and concluded that the fight was 'a Balinese reading of Balinese experience; a story they tell themselves about themselves'.[53]

The return of narrative was not confined to academic disciplines but also affected everyday life outside the academy. Take the case of the law, for example, especially in the United States, where what is known as the 'legal storytelling movement' developed in the 1980s, associated once again with an increasing concern with ordinary people and the ways in which they make sense of their lives. In similar fashion, an increasing interest in stories in medical circles is associated with a greater concern for the patient's point of view, with the idea that, in some respects, people know and understand their own bodies and their own illnesses better than outsiders, even if these outsiders are qualified doctors.

As often happens with revivals, the new narratives differ from the old ones in important respects. Historical narratives, for instance, used to be Olympian, as if the historian was looking down on events from a distance, like the so-called 'omniscient narrator' of many nineteenth-century novels. In contrast, the new narratives often present a variety of voices or points of view, following the model of *Rashomon* (1950), the famous film by the Japanese director Akira Kurosawa (based on two short stories by a writer of the early twentieth century, Ryunosuke Akutagawa), recounting contradictory versions of an incident leading to a murder. Whatever the intentions of Akutagawa or Kurosawa may have been, current concern among anthropologists and sociologists with what they call the 'Rashomon Effect' is to use stories as a means to reconstruct the attitudes and values of the tellers, moving from a conflict of narratives to a narrative of conflicts.[54]

Disseminating Knowledges

The rise of newspapers was not only an encouragement to scepticism but also a watershed in the dissemination of knowledge, the third stage in our four-stage sequence. Dissemination is sometimes described, especially in the case of technology, as 'transfer', emphasizing movement in one direction. Other scholars prefer to speak of the 'circulation' of knowledge, an assumption that is often more realistic. Interest in the movement or transit of knowledges has increased sharply in the last few years, as a number of important studies bear witness.[55] Whether we call it transfer or circulation, we need of course to remember that knowledge received is not the same as knowledge sent, owing to misunderstandings (a relatively neglected part of intellectual history) as well as to deliberate adaptations or cultural translations.

It is easy, all too easy, to tell the story of dissemination in 'triumphalist' fashion, as a story of more and more knowledge reaching more and more people thanks to increasingly efficient methods of communication – writing, print, the radio, television and the internet. The general problems raised by triumphalist accounts will be discussed in Chapter 4. Here it may be sufficient to make two points, one about dissemination in general, and the second about forms of communication.

In the first place, there is a long tradition of critics of the dissemination or 'democratization' of knowledge. In early modern Europe, for instance, the clergy were uncomfortable with the idea of the laity reading the Bible for themselves, masters of specialist knowledge, from goldsmiths to physicians, objected to the publication of their secrets, while rulers and their advisers saw the spread of knowledge as a threat to the hierarchical social order.

In the second place, even scholars have expressed anxiety about what we now call 'information overload'. In the fourteenth century, the historian Ibn Khaldun was already complaining that 'the great number of works available' was 'among the things that are harmful to the human quest for knowledge'. Anxiety of this kind became more widespread in the West a century or so after Gutenberg printed his first book.[56]

In any case, despite the importance of new forms of communication, the most effective means of dissemination remains the oldest one, encounters with people. It has been argued that 'the transfer of really valuable knowledge from country to country or from institution to institution cannot be easily achieved by the transport of letters, journals and books: it necessitates the physical movement of human beings'. In short, 'ideas move around inside people'.[57]

Oral transmission

Movements of people include those of students and teachers. The history of education is a long-established part of what is now known as the history of knowledge, with many studies of individual schools and universities and some important overviews.[58] As a case-study we might take education in the traditional Islamic world, as presented in books about medieval Cairo and Damascus written by the American historians Jonathan Berkey and Michael Chamberlain. In these cities, the system of higher education was essentially an informal one. The *madrasas*, schools attached to mosques, offered students stipends, accommodation and lectures, but the most important path to knowledge was to become the disciple of a master or *shaykh*. According to a twelfth-century treatise, it was 'essential that the pupils sit in a semi-circle at a certain distance from the teacher', as a mark of respect.

In this informal system there was no fixed curriculum. The equivalent of a Western degree, the *ijaza*, a licence to teach, was conferred by the *shaykh* following an oral examination. 'Students built their careers on the reputation of their teachers.' The system was also an open one in the sense that it gave women the opportunity to learn from other women in sessions in private houses. Reading (especially the Koran), copying and writing books were also important activities, but students were supposed to read aloud in a group. Private study was frowned on and books were considered an inferior method of transmitting knowledge. The fourteenth-century jurist Ibn Jama'a declared that 'One of the greatest calamities is taking texts as *shaykhs*' and that 'knowledge is not gained from books'.[59]

Close relations between masters and 'disciples' can be found in Western culture too, to this day.[60] However, they were and are part of a larger system for transmitting knowledge that originated in the Middle Ages: the university. Medieval universities relied heavily on the spoken word, in lectures and also in the formal debates known as 'disputations' in which students practised and developed their logical skills. By contrast with the Islamic world of learning, however, writing also had an important place in the system. Lecturers, as their name implies, read texts aloud to students, and the students in their turn wrote down what they heard. Reading and writing gradually became more important at the expense of listening and speaking. All the same, oral communication remains important in Western academic culture even today, as Françoise Waquet has reminded us in a history of lectures, seminars and conferences.[61]

Performing knowledge

Oral transmission may be described as 'performance'. Virtuoso performers already existed at the University of Paris in the twelfth century, notably Peter Abelard, who attracted many students to his lectures and – perhaps equally important for him – away from the lectures of his competitors. In the sixteenth century, the Swiss physician Paracelsus drew attention to himself at the University of Basel by a public burning of the traditional medical treatises that he rejected. An eighteenth-century German professor, Burckhardt Mencke, criticized professors who played to the gallery in his book *Charlataneria Eruditorum* ('The Charlatanry of the Learned', 1715), a book that went through several editions in Latin and translation as well as inspiring imitations. Mencke compared these academics to the charlatans who performed on stages in the street in order to sell their medicines, pointing out the tricks to which scholars resorted to gain applause – wearing expensive or eccentric clothes or lecturing with 'vehement expressions, constant changes of countenance, rude and wandering eyes, whirling arms, shifting feet, suggestive movements of the hips and other parts of the body'.

Had he lived a little longer, Mencke would have been able to make significant additions to his list. From the later eighteenth century onwards, experiments were regularly presented in public as spectacles, a kind of theatre with the lecturer as the showman. Chemistry lent itself to showmanship of this kind and so did electricity, the words of the lecturer being accompanied by flashes and bangs. At Oxford, the eccentric geologist-palaeontologist William Buckland enlivened his presentations by imitating the movements of dinosaurs. In London, John Henry Pepper, a nineteenth-century lecturer on science, was a famous deviser of what would now be called 'special effects', such as making ghosts appear on the stage. Today's television dons are the heirs of a long tradition.[62]

Testing knowledge

How to test the knowledge that students have acquired is another old problem. Asking them to perform their knowledge in public is an obvious solution, taking different forms; participation in debates, delivering speeches or answering a series of questions. An alternative method is the one that most of us now take for granted. It is the written examination, invented in China and studied by sinologists such as John Chaffee and Benjamin Elman.[63]

For about a thousand years, from the early Song to the late Qing dynasty, China was administered by the group known in the West as 'mandarins', scholar-officials who owed their appointment and so their social status to success in written examinations. The examinations were central to the traditional Chinese knowledge order, and to the social order as well. Records of dreams about examinations suggest that they were central to Chinese culture more generally. The examinations were usually held every three years at the provincial level, and then, for successful candidates, at the national level. They lasted three days. The candidates sat in individual cubicles in the examination hall, writing essays – commentaries on the Confucian classics, such as the *Great Learning* or the *Doctrine of the Mean*, which were regarded as sources of wisdom and virtue, but also essays on questions of policy, questions of law, and sometimes on questions of astronomy (over this long period, the suitability of different fields of knowledge for these examinations was debated, and changes were made). The examiners did not know the identity of the candidates whom they graded.

Long years of study were required for success in these examinations, although the survival of printed guides and model essays suggests that many candidates attempted to take short cuts. Some of these printed guides were very small, for smuggling into the examination hall, hidden in one's robes. Despite the possibility of successful cheating, the system was probably the most efficient system of testing knowledge in the pre-industrial world, so that it is no surprise to find that it was imitated in the West, first in eighteenth-century Prussia and then in France, England and elsewhere. In Oxford and Cambridge, for instance, written examinations were introduced in the early nineteenth century, replacing the oral system known as examination *viva voce*, 'by the living voice'. In the mid nineteenth century, written examinations on the Chinese model were introduced to test candidates for the British civil service. This may be the reason that senior civil servants are still described as 'mandarins'.[64]

Sending missions

Knowledge has often been transmitted by missionaries, whether they were Buddhist, Christian or Muslim. The story of the spread of Buddhism, for instance, is a story of long-distance travel, from India to Sri Lanka, Burma, Thailand, Laos, Cambodia and China and from China to Korea and Japan. The main agents of dissemination were monks. For example, Jianzhen was a Buddhist priest from Tang-dynasty China who spent the last ten years of his life in Japan, where (known as Ganjin) he founded a school and a temple and introduced the Japanese aristocracy to the doctrines of the Buddha. Ganjin's story, told by one of his disciples in the *Record of the Eastward Journey of the Great Monk of Tang*, was retold by the Japanese novelist Yashushi Inoué in *The Roof Tile of Tempyō* (1957) from a Japanese point of view, focusing on the official mission to China that set out in the year 732, taking monks to study Buddhism there. As described in the novel, the mission included four young monks who persuaded Ganjin to come to Japan.

Ganjin also introduced the Japanese to secular elements of Chinese culture. Missionaries often disseminate secular knowledge in this way. Indeed, in the nineteenth century in particular, Christian missionaries in Asia, Africa and elsewhere often considered it part of their task to introduce the peoples among whom they worked to Western culture and especially to Western science. For example, John Fryer, a Protestant missionary, founded the *Chinese Scientific Magazine* (1876) and set up a polytechnic in Shanghai, while another missionary, Alexander Williamson, founded the Society for the Diffusion of Christian and General Knowledge among the Chinese, a society that published scientific books as well as religious ones. Missionaries often founded colleges that disseminated Western learning; the Syrian Protestant College (1866), for instance, St Stephen's College Delhi (1881), Canton Christian College (1888) and so on.

Conversely, missionaries studied the languages and cultures of the regions in which they worked, and when they returned home they often spread the knowledge of those regions. In this respect missionaries have sometimes been compared to anthropologists. Indeed, a few of them ended their careers as anthropologists. A famous example is that of Maurice Leenhardt, a French Protestant pastor in New Caledonia, which had become a French possession in 1853. After working there from 1902 to 1927, Leenhardt returned to France, where he taught at the École Pratique des Hautes Etudes and elsewhere as an expert on Melanesia.[65]

Missionaries were not alone in travelling to disseminate knowledges. There were secular missions as well. On one side, some Western countries, notably France, sent missions abroad, such as the group of young scholars (including Fernand Braudel and Claude Lévi-Strauss) who were sent to the University of São Paulo in the 1930s. On the other side, governments that considered their country to be backward sent knowledge-finding missions to more 'progressive' countries. For example, the Egyptian government sent a group of students to France in 1826, including the young Rifa'a al-Tatawi, who became a leading Islamic modernizer.[66] Again, in 1862 the Japanese government sent a mission to Europe to learn about Western civilization (it may be suspected that the novelist Inoué was thinking of this event when he described the mission to China sent in 732).

Indian encounters

Besides missions, informal encounters led to the transmission of knowledges. One famous series of examples concerns the Dutch East India Company, the VOC. Some Dutchmen, Germans and Swedes in the service of the Company took the opportunity to study both nature and culture in Japan and South East Asia, and to write books that spread that knowledge in Europe. Something similar happened in India in the late eighteenth and early nineteenth centuries, the age when the British East India Company effectively ruled much of the country. Some administrators, judges, physicians and surgeons in the service of the Company studied the history, languages and local knowledges of the places in which they served, learning from local scholars and spreading Western knowledges in return, each side adapting what they learned to their own purposes. Appropriately enough, the history of these encounters and exchanges has been written jointly by Western and by Indian scholars.[67]

The most famous example of this kind of intellectual exchange is surely that of the Welsh lawyer William Jones, who arrived in Calcutta in 1783, founded the Asiatic Society of Bengal, conversed regularly with local scholars (the *pandits*), discovered that Greek and Latin derived from Sanskrit, and introduced Europe to the Sanskrit drama *Sakuntala* through his English translation. In similar fashion, the identification of the 'Dravidian' family of languages in South India was the result of the 'conversation' between British and Indian scholars.[68] In the field of medicine, a number of physicians and surgeons in the service of the Company, many of them Scottish, exchanged knowledge with local healers from the Ayurvedic and other traditions. On the other side, in nineteenth-century Bengal, societies were founded by Indian elites who were enthusiastic for Western science: the Society for the Acquisition of General Knowledge (1838), for instance, or the Indian Society for the Cultivation of Science (1876).[69]

The significance of these exchanges of knowledge remains a matter of debate. Inspired by Michel Foucault and Edward Said, whose work was discussed in Chapter 2, some scholars emphasize the conflict between knowledges, notoriously illustrated by the disqualification of traditional Indian knowledge by Thomas Macaulay, who served on the Supreme Council in India from 1834 to 1838 and claimed in his 'Minute on Indian Education' that 'a single shelf of a good European library was worth the whole native literature of India and Arabia'. These scholars note the political uses of knowledge in the service of either British imperialism or, later, Indian nationalism, as in the case of Jadu Nath Ganguli's *National System of Medicine in India* (1911), arguing that India needed a 'system of medicine on national lines'.

In contrast, other scholars stress the harmony of different knowledge orders and the fascination exerted by foreign knowledge, in the case of both Europeans who discovered Indian traditions and Indians who discovered Western science. As Thomas Trautmann argues, studies of the 'formation of colonial knowledge' 'need to consider the kinds of knowledge that were brought *to* the colonial situation, from *both* parties to the colonial relation'.[70] The problem, then, is to assess the relative importance of Western and Indian contributions, as well as to try to navigate between the two extremes of a political approach to knowledge that risks becoming cynical and reductionist and a non-political approach that runs the danger of naivety.

Displacement

In the history of knowledge as in history in general, unintended consequences have often been more important than intended ones. More influential than missions in either direction were the experiences of expatriates such as Jones or the travels of scholars who would have preferred not to leave home but were forced to do so, like the Protestants who were expelled from France in 1685 and settled in London, Berlin and the Dutch Republic, or the Jewish scholars who left Germany in 1933 or Austria in 1938 for Britain, the United States and elsewhere.[71] The problems of the broken lives of these displaced persons are obvious enough. However, some individuals at least were able to gain a living as mediators between their home culture and the culture that received them. French Protestants in England wrote on English history or translated English books, including the philosophy of John Locke, into French, while German Jewish scholars in the United States translated Max Weber's sociology into English. Again, some scholars who left Russia after 1917 spent the remainder of their working lives explaining Russian culture to the French, British and Americans.

For their hosts, the positive side to this displacement is easier to track, especially when there were enough refugees in a particular discipline and a particular place to constitute a critical mass, introducing psychoanalysis into the United States, for example, or art history into England.[72] As in other cases of the migration of skilled people, like the Protestant silk-weavers who left France along with the scholars, one nation was enriched by the losses of another.

Disseminating through objects

Objects such as rocks, plants, stuffed animals, paintings and statues disseminated knowledge as they moved from one part of the world to another and entered collections, for study as well as for display. In early modern Europe, these collections were private, owned by rulers such as the Medici in Florence or by scholars such as the Danish physician Ole Worm. They included works of art alongside works of nature, European coins and medals, Mexican feather-work or Brazilian blow-pipes together with shells or crocodiles. Since the French Revolution, public collections have become the dominant form, displayed in museums and galleries and open to visitors, often including schoolchildren. Viewing these objects has become part of many people's education. Indeed, some museums were established for educational purposes, like the South Kensington Museum in London (founded in 1857 in order to show artisans what models they might follow), or the Science Museum that split off from it in 1885.

The transport of texts also disseminated knowledge. Japanese monks returned from their time in China with thousands of scrolls of Buddhist texts, many of them copied by themselves. The rise of paper (much cheaper than parchment) in China, the Islamic world and finally in Europe contributed to the spread of knowledge in the age of manuscript. The invention of printing with moveable type made books more easily available and at a lower price than before. Books were already travelling long distances in the sixteenth century, from Spain, for instance, to Mexico or Peru. So were letters (although they might take a long time to arrive at their destinations), thus creating long-distance networks of knowledge, between Jesuit scholars in Rome, Goa and Beijing for instance, or, more generally, extending the frontiers of the so-called 'Republic of Letters'.[73]

Constructing the Republic of Letters

The Republic of Letters may be regarded as an imagined community, a college without walls or a network of networks. Most studies of this community begin in the fifteenth century, when the phrase *respublica litterarum* was coined, and come to an end around the year 1800, when the unity of the Republic was threatened first by nationalism and then by intellectual specialization.

However, a case can be made for extending its history to our own time, distinguishing between four main periods on the basis of changes in modes of communication.[74] The first age, from about 1500 to 1800, was that of the horse-drawn republic, when books, letters and scholars themselves all needed horse-power in order to travel on land, and sailing-ships to cross the seas. The second age, 1800–1950, was the age of what we might call the 'steam republic'. The steam press drove down the price of books, while the railways and the steamships allowed international conferences to become regular events where scholars could exchange information.

In the third age, more or less 1950–90, the growing ease of air travel encouraged the proliferation of small international conferences on specific themes. Today we are living in a fourth age, that of the 'digital republic'. The Republic of Letters was always a virtual or imagined community, but the acceleration of communication, thanks to e-mail, e-conferencing, and collective e-research, has made its members more conscious of interaction at a distance than they used to be and given a new meaning to the old idea of an 'invisible college'.

Thanks to changes in communication, the Republic of Letters, originally confined to Western Europe, was gradually extended, to the Balkans, Russia and to some cities in the Americas, North and South, and later to other parts of the world, leading to the movement of knowledges on a global scale. Already in the eighteenth century, thanks to faster sailing-ships, the former students, known as the 'apostles' of the Swedish botanist Carl Linnaeus, were able to send him information from the Middle East, Africa, China, North and South America and (in the case of Solander, who sailed with Banks and Cook) Australia.

Offering a simple three-stage model of the diffusion of scientific knowledge, George Basalla once argued that as in the case of international trade, the periphery exported raw material, such as the information gathered by Western scientific expeditions to other parts of the world, while the centre (in this case the 'centres of calculation' in the West) exported finished products. Only at a later third stage did the production of scientific knowledge spread outside the centres.[75] Recent studies have continued to emphasize the links between Western science and Western imperialism, noting for example that 'The emergence of centres of science, such as museums, gardens, asylums and universities depended on the passage of data, material culture and people across imperial networks.'[76]

Basalla was writing in the 1960s and since that time his model has often been criticized, especially for three reasons. In the first place, knowledge as well as information moves from the periphery to the centre as well as vice versa. For example, the sixteenth-century Portuguese physician García de Orta, who published a famous study of Indian medicinal herbs in 1563, drew on the local knowledge of Indian healers.[77] In the second place, exotic knowledge is domesticated on both sides of the exchange. In other words, it is translated from one language to another and subjected to 'cultural translation' in the sense of being adapted to a new environment, producing what has been called hybrid or 'pidgin-knowledge'. Hence the need felt by scholars today to go 'beyond diffusionism'.[78]

In the third place, thinking of knowledges in the plural, it is clear that different knowledges had their own centres. Basalla's model of the spread of Western science naturally privileged Western centres, but a model of the spread of Indian or Chinese knowledges would privilege Indian or Chinese centres for equally good reasons. In any case, the model could and should be refined, as suggested in Chapter 2, by introducing the idea of the 'semi-periphery', including colonial cities such as sixteenth-century Goa, where García de Orta lived, conversed with Indian healers and wrote his book, or eighteenth-century Bombay or Calcutta, where British doctors and surgeons in the service of the East India Company learned from their Indian colleagues as well as teaching them.[79] Again, the Japanese port city of Nagasaki, including the small island of Deshima where Western traders were confined from the seventeenth to the nineteenth centuries, became a centre for both the Western discovery of Japan and the Japanese discovery of Europe. As the nineteenth-century journalist Fujita Mokichi remarked, 'Nagasaki was not simply a place for trade in goods with the Dutch, it was also a new port for trade in knowledge.'[80]

Translating knowledges

Needless to say, these exchanges of knowledges required the participation of interpreters and translators between languages. What is sometimes called 'cultural translation' also took place, with both sides adapting what they had learned to their own needs and circumstances. What was often, though not always, 'lost in translation' was what turned that information into knowledge, local classification systems, for instance. The loss is worth bearing in mind when we consider the importance of translation between languages for the spread of knowledge. As has already been noted, the spread of Buddhism from India to China and Japan involved translation between three very different languages: Sanskrit, Chinese and Japanese. Again, much ancient Greek knowledge, especially knowledge of the natural world, reached Western Europe via the Arabs. Translations of Aristotle, for instance, were made from Greek into Arabic and later from Arabic into Latin and sometimes from Latin into French and other vernaculars, so that a text by 'Aristotle' might be the translation of a translation of a translation of a text, many times transcribed, of what Aristotle himself had dictated.

In any case, Aristotle's world of small city-republics was very different from the medieval Europe dominated by the Church and by kings, so that the ideas put forward in his *Politics*, for instance, were often misunderstood. Indeed, one might argue that these ideas needed to be misunderstood in order to be relevant to the fourteenth- or fifteenth-century world in which they were read. In other words, these ideas passed through a process of cultural translation as well as a translation from one language to another.[81] The process of the cultural translation of knowledge is even clearer in the case of some non-verbal examples, like the maps made by the Inuit at the moment of their encounter with Europeans in the late eighteenth century, thus documenting 'a search for cross-cultural equivalences'.[82] As discussions of this example suggest, historians have moved from dismissing non-Western maps as inaccurate to viewing them as evidence of different understandings of space.

Popularization

The dissemination of knowledge takes place not only laterally, spreading across space, but also vertically, moving from scientists, scholars and other experts to the 'lay' public. Movements for the popularization of knowledge, especially certain kinds of knowledge, have a long history. In Britain, for instance, the Society for the Promotion of Christian Knowledge was founded in 1698.

The dissemination of knowledge to the laity, including women and children, has been the subject of a number of important recent studies. The studies focus on Germany, France and especially on Victorian England, where the phrase 'popularizer of science' was in use by 1848.[83] One mode of dissemination was the public lecture, which sometime drew crowds, as in the case of Alexander von Humboldt's lectures on the cosmos, given in Berlin (1827–8), or Max Müller's lectures on language at the Royal Institution in London (1861). Another was the museum. A third mode of dissemination was of course print. From the sixteenth century onwards, books on medicine with titles such as 'Medicine for the Common Man' or 'Treasury of Health' were published in vernacular languages, allowing readers to avoid the expense of calling in a physician by practising 'do it yourself' healing. Some of them went through many editions.

Books disseminating other kinds of knowledge might also become best-sellers. John Hawkesworth, the author of an account of Cook's first voyage, commissioned by the Admiralty and published in 1773, is supposed to have received an advance of six thousand pounds from the publisher, a huge amount for the time, suggesting that the book was expected to sell very well. The anonymous *Vestiges of the Natural History of Creation* (1844, actually written by Robert Chambers) appealed to readers both high and low in the social scale.[84] A similar point may be made about Macaulay's *History of England* (1848). Three thousand copies of the first volume were sold in less than a fortnight, while a group of working men from near Manchester wrote to the author to thank him for writing the book, which had been read aloud to them on Wednesday evenings. Magazines also helped to spread knowledge: *The Scientific American* (founded in 1845), for instance, the *Chinese Scientific Magazine* (founded by an English missionary, 1876) or the *National Geographic Magazine* (1888).

In different periods, from antiquity onwards, and in different cultures (especially European, Islamic and East Asian) knowledge has been disseminated by means of what we call 'encyclopaedias', volumes great or small that claim to contain within their pages, if not all knowledge, then at least the essentials. Encyclopaedias are the best-known of the many types of book, including specialist works such as dictionaries or guides to practices such as cooking or horsemanship, that are designed not to be read from cover to cover but to be consulted whenever needed. From the sixteenth century onwards, reference books in general and encyclopaedias in particular proliferated both in the West and in East Asia. By the mid eighteenth century, there were so many of them that an enterprising Frenchman produced a *Dictionary of Dictionaries*.[85]

A recent study of the consequences of the popularization of knowledge is Mary Elizabeth Berry's *Japan in Print*, focusing on the early Tokugawa period, better known to Westerners as the seventeenth century, when the rise of cities, especially Kyoto, Osaka and Edo (now Tokyo), was accompanied by the rise of printed books targeting an increasingly wide public – women as well as men, farmers as well as artisans and shopkeepers. Many of the books printed for this public or for part of it provided information. Guides to Edo and Kyoto, for instance, told visitors what to see, from temples to teahouses, and where to go in search of different goods and services. Instruction manuals gave advice on how to farm, to write letters or poems, to perform the tea ceremony and to bring up children. Cheap encyclopaedias such as *Banmin chohoki* ('Everybody's Treasury', 1692) made their appearance. This 'library of public information', as Berry calls it, encouraged a 'revolution in knowledge' and led to the rise of a public sphere, an arena for the discussion of public issues, while the publication of maps of Japan helped widen imagined communities from regions to the whole country.[86]

Censoring

A discussion of the dissemination of knowledge needs to take account of the complementary opposite theme of the obstacles to this dissemination. Economic obstacles, for instance, such as the cost of books, including that of transporting them over long distances, not to mention the so-called 'tax on knowledge', as the stamp duty on British newspapers came to be known (imposed in 1712, the stamp duty was finally abolished in 1855). Deliberate censorship of communication also has a long history. The spread of printed books in particular has been viewed unfavourably by many authorities, religious and secular. In Japan, in the age of the 'library of public information', books were censored by the government. In China, the tradition of censorship goes back as far as the third century BCE but is best known from the time of the emperor Qianlong in the late eighteenth century, when edicts against 'seditious books' and 'heterodox opinions' were issued in response to the 'flood' of printed texts.[87]

In early modern Europe, the censorship of printed books was a major preoccupation of the authorities in both states and churches, Protestant and Catholic alike, whether their anxieties concerned heresy, sedition, or immorality. The most famous and widespread censorship system of the period was that of the Catholic Church, associated with the 'Index of Prohibited Books'. This Index was a printed catalogue of the books that the faithful were forbidden to read, an antidote to the poisons of print and Protestantism. The important indices were those issued by papal authority and binding on the whole Catholic Church, from the mid sixteenth century to the mid twentieth century.[88] Bonfires of books could often be seen in the Catholic world: bonfires of Muslim books in sixteenth-century Spain, or of Protestant books in Antwerp, Paris, Florence, Venice and other cities. Protestant censorship was less effective than Catholic censorship not because the Protestants were more tolerant but because they were more divided, fragmented into Lutherans, Calvinists and so on.

Government censorship of books before publication came to an end in England in 1695, in France in 1789, in Prussia in 1850 and in Russia in 1905. All the same, attempts to control what was published did not disappear. Book-burning continued: a notorious example is a series of bonfires in different German cities of books by Jewish, Communist or foreign authors, events organized by the German Students' Union in 1933, soon after Hitler came to power. Today, authoritarian regimes in Iran, Russia and elsewhere ban books, control television programmes and block access to certain websites on the Internet, as in the case of the so-called 'golden shield' or 'great firewall of China', which was launched in the year 2000.

Concealment and revelation

Just as historians need to study ignorance as the complementary opposite of knowledge, so they need to study concealment as the opposite of diffusion. Rulers have long attempted to preserve the *arcana imperii*, 'secrets of state'. The subjects of imperial regimes may try to conceal local knowledge from their new masters. Eighteenth-century Hindu scholars, for example, tried to prevent the British from learning Sanskrit.[89] Secret societies attempt to restrict certain knowledges to the circle of the initiated. Specialists, from smiths to masters of ceremonies, do the same, in order to preserve their intellectual capital. It is no accident that the English word 'mystery' used to refer to crafts as well as secrets.

As may be imagined, however, serious problems of method arise for historians working in this domain. Failed concealment is obviously easier to study than the success that hides its traces. All the same, the failures offer insights into changing strategies and methods of concealment in the long conflict between the defenders, in other words the individuals, groups and institutions that try to keep certain knowledges secret, and their opponents, who try to gain access either for themselves or for a wider public, often assisted by 'moles' inside the system. As in the case of wars, new methods of defence respond to new methods of attack, apparently *ad infinitum*.

The different stages in this long conflict between concealment and discovery are more visible than usual in the history of codes and ciphers. In the ninth century, the Arab philosopher al-Kindi wrote a guide to decipherment. In the fifteenth century, polyalphabetic ciphers were invented to prevent decipherment by an analysis of the frequency with which certain letters recurred. In the nineteenth century, a more sophisticated mathematical analysis led to the breaking of polyalphabetic ciphers. The twentieth century was the age of cipher machines such the famous Enigma, with a code that was broken by the joint efforts of Polish cryptographers and a British team located in Bletchley Park.[90] In the age of the Internet, we see both new forms of attack such as automated intelligence gathering, and new forms of defence such as automated security systems.

Another example of this conflict concerns the collection of information by means of surveillance, secret information that is 'leaked' to the public from time to time. On one side, we see the efforts of governments, or more recently of large corporations, to gather information and keep it to themselves. In early modern Venice, for instance, ambassadors resident in other states used spies and other informers to collect sensitive information, which went into their confidential reports. Today, the work of spies (known in the jargon as HUMINT, 'human intelligence') has been supplemented if not replaced by TECHINT, 'technical intelligence'. Take the case of the NSA, the National Security Agency of the USA, which collects and even analyses data by means of programmes such as XKeyscore, which searches for information on the Internet (including private e-mails). In industry as well as in politics, espionage has moved from the infiltration of organizations by individuals to the hacking of computers from a distance.

On the other side, historians have discovered that the confidential reports of Venetian ambassadors were often copied and the copies sold in Rome and elsewhere. Filippo De Vivo tells the story of an early seventeenth-century Venetian diplomat who had been posted to England and was shocked to discover, in the Bodleian Library in Oxford, 'a large volume in manuscript' that contained fourteen of these reports.[91] The recent history of the revelation of official secrets includes a number of episodes in which individuals inside the system supplied information in electronic form; Bradley Manning (as he then was) sent US Air Force documents concerning the war in Iraq to Wikileaks in 2010, while Edward Snowden sent copies of NSA documents to the *Guardian* and the *Washington Post* in 2013. The media of communication change, and so does the amount of information in circulation, but the old conflict between secrecy and transparency continues.

Gaining access

Attempts to keep information secret and attempts to reveal it (whether by moles, journalists or hackers) both raise the question of access, since secrecy presupposes insiders who know the secret as well as outsiders who are excluded. Access to knowledge has long been unequal, especially access to knowledge-creating and knowledge-storing institutions such as universities, archives, libraries and museums. Attempts to widen this access also have a long history. Five hundred years ago, print became a major instrument in these attempts. However, print could not widen access to knowledge by itself. Two obstacles had to be overcome: illiteracy and Latin. Hence the movements, one might even say the campaigns, to spread literacy and to make knowledges available in vernacular languages.

Martin Luther, a fellow-countryman of Gutenberg's, was a leader and has become the symbol of the collective attempt to make religious knowledge, especially knowledge of the Bible, available in the vernacular, an attempt that was central to the movement that we now call the Reformation. In the case of medicine, the role of Luther was played by another German, Paracelsus, who insisted on both lecturing and writing in the vernacular.

In the long term, the movement for what we might call the vernacularization of knowledges was impossible to resist. Until the first half of the seventeenth century, printed encyclopaedias usually appeared in Latin, but after that time they were replaced by encyclopaedias in modern languages, among them the Scottish *Encyclopaedia Britannica* and the famous French *Encyclopédie*. The *Encyclopédie* made another important and controversial contribution to making knowledges more common. It described the practices of many types of artisan in rich detail, with many illustrations. In this way it introduced to a wider public a number of knowledges that had previously been kept from the uninitiated. Making private knowledges public in this way was part of Diderot's campaign against the guild system. He believed that this 'publicization' of craft knowledge would make the economy prosper and benefit humanity.[92]

The ideal of common knowledge took institutional form in nineteenth-century societies such as the British Society for the Diffusion of Useful Knowledge (founded 1826, following similar initiatives in Germany and the USA); in educational institutions for adults such as Mechanics' Institutes, as they used to be called in Britain, or 'People's High Schools'

(*Folkehøjskole*), as they were known in Denmark; and also in popular encyclopaedias such as the one published in Britain in 1860 by the Chambers brothers, subtitled 'A Dictionary of Universal Knowledge for the People'. The popular newspaper, aimed at a wide audience, is another nineteenth-century invention that spread rapidly in the USA, Britain, France, Germany and elsewhere. It depended on the earlier spread of literacy, thanks to universal or almost universal education (in England, from 1870 onwards, at almost exactly the same time as in Japan, where a campaign for modernization was just beginning). It might be argued that parliamentary democracy depended on that invention, which gave ordinary voters the information they needed to make a political choice. As the Liberal Chancellor of the Exchequer, Robert Lowe, remarked in his sardonic manner at the time that the right to vote was extended in England in 1867, 'We must educate our masters.'

In the twentieth century, at least three revolutions in technology widened access to some knowledges and indeed made the dream of a common knowledge seem attainable at last: radio, television and the internet. The globalization of knowledges was aided by the spread of English as an international medium of communication, a kind of new Latin, as well as by the spread of images that need no translation. The second half of the twentieth century was also the great age of the democratization of knowledges, thanks in part to radio lectures, televised science, open universities and online encyclopaedias. In the political domain, there were movements for increased freedom of information or transparency in government. *Glasnost* was promoted by Mikhail Gorbachev soon after he came to power in 1985. This meant reducing 'the number of officially forbidden topics' in the press.[93] Elsewhere freedom of information acts have gone much further and given the public access to official documents.

So far the examples cited concern knowledges that have become increasingly common. All the same, it is necessary to avoid the assumption of the inevitable spread of knowledges, whether geographically or socially. It is more realistic to view the history of knowledges as a kind of tug of war, a conflict between the forces for widening and the forces for narrowing access. To write in a vernacular language was to widen access to many knowledges in one way, by making them available to social groups that had not learned Latin. However, writing in a vernacular narrowed access in another way, access for foreigners. In Luther's time, Erasmus wrote his books in Latin in order to reach a European audience from England to Poland. His audience was wide geographically but narrow socially, while Luther's was the reverse. Again, paradoxically enough, globalization restricts access to knowledges as well as widening it. It narrows access to zero by destroying some knowledges altogether. Many local knowledges are in crisis, a crisis that may indeed be terminal. To take one of the most obvious examples, many of the world's languages, of which there are about six thousand currently spoken, are in danger of extinction by the end of the twenty-first century, if not before.

In any case, the conquest of access has always been under threat. There were and are three major threats. The first and perhaps the least obvious threat comes from intellectual specialization. Collectively we know much more than ever before but individually we all find it harder and harder to see the big picture. The second threat to common knowledge comes from political regimes. The threat takes two main forms: the negative form of censorship and the positive form of secret or restricted knowledges, generally associated with authoritarian states but in fact virtually ubiquitous, even if in different degrees. The third threat to common knowledge is the trend towards privatization. The idea of the ownership of knowledge is not an invention of capitalism, but the privatization of knowledges has been much extended by capitalists via patents and other forms of intellectual property. For example, pharmaceutical companies have tried to patent traditional indigenous knowledges such as the antiseptic properties of the Indian spice turmeric.

Stewart Brand, best known as the author of the *Whole Earth Catalog*, coined the phrase 'information wants to be free'. More cautiously, the economist Kenneth Arrow remarked that 'it is difficult to make information into property'.[94] All the same, some governments and some companies have succeeded, at least temporarily, in this task.

Employing Knowledges

'Useful knowledge' has long been a widespread slogan, the focus of organizations and campaigns from the middle of the eighteenth century onwards. In Erfurt, the 'Academy of Useful Knowledges' (Akademie gemeinütziger Wissenschaften) was founded in 1754. In Philadelphia, the American Philosophical Society for the Promotion of Useful Knowledge dates from 1766 and was followed by similar societies in Trenton, New York, Lexington and elsewhere. In Britain, the Society for the Diffusion of Useful Knowledge was founded in 1826. In France, the *Journal des Connaissances utiles* was established in 1832.

It is of course necessary to ask: useful to whom, or for what? Different knowledges have obviously been employed for many purposes. In early modern Europe, for instance, the study of classical rhetoric was of practical use in the domains of law and politics. Empires could hardly survive without access to detailed knowledge of the terrain and its resources. Geographical knowledge has also been deployed in warfare. Hence the use of topographical engineers in Napoleon's armies, for instance, surveying and mapping Austria, Italy and Russia. Later in the nineteenth century it was the turn of the Prussians, whose victory in the war with France in 1870–1 was described by a geographer as 'a war fought as much by maps as by weapons'. Since the Gulf War (1990–1), armies have been making use of Geographical Information Systems.

In business as in war, it is as important to discover the plans and the technology of one's competitors as to keep one's own plans and technology secret. In short, knowledge is often employed in the service of control, a point emphasized by Foucault in his famous statement, quoted earlier in this book, that 'knowledge constantly induces effects of power'.

The Counter-Reformation Church

Foucault's point may be illustrated from the history of the Catholic Church at the time of the so-called 'Counter-

Reformation' of the sixteenth and seventeenth centuries. The spread of Protestantism administered a kind of wake-up call to the authorities, to which they responded in various ways. In the first place, the Church made greater efforts than before to spread religious knowledge among ordinary people by means of sermons and also, a novelty, by means of catechism classes. The question-and-answer format of the catechism made it easier to test religious knowledge. In the second place, there were systematic attempts on the part of bishops to acquire information about religious practice. To ensure that no one failed to go to confession, censuses were made in each diocese. Bishops were also supposed to conduct 'visitations', in other words inspections of each parish, ranging from the physical state of the parish church and its fittings to the behaviour and beliefs of the laity (whether there were any heretics, how many people had been excommunicated or were living with concubines). Standardized questionnaires were issued to allow the information from different sources to be compared.[95]

In Spain, Italy, Portugal and the Catholic parts of the New World, the efforts of the bishops were seconded by those of the Inquisition, which investigated both belief and behaviour and accumulated over the centuries an impressive 'data bank' that is now regularly raided by historians for their own purposes. Among the new religious orders founded during the Counter-Reformation were the Jesuits, an order that grew very rapidly in numbers and established itself in mission fields in many parts of the world, from Canada to Paraguay and from India to Japan. One distinctive feature of the organization of the Jesuits was the extent and the sophistication of their information system. They were a centralized order, ruled by a 'general' in Rome, to whom was addressed a series of regular reports or 'annual letters' from Jesuit houses and colleges all over the world, thus allowing him to keep a close watch on what was happening in each location and to extend 'a long arm' wherever and whenever this became necessary.[96]

Among Protestants too, the clergy was concerned both with spreading religious knowledge among ordinary people and with acquiring knowledge about them. The first point may be illustrated from the history of two British societies, the Society for the Promotion of Christian Knowledge (SPCK), founded in 1698 to support missionaries, and the British and Foreign Bible Society, founded in 1804 to make the Bible more easily available throughout the world. As for the second point, Protestants like Catholics carried out visitations. In Sweden from the seventeenth century onwards, the clergy made regular visits to the houses of the laity to test all the family members on their ability both to read and to understand the Bible.[97]

Bureaucratization

The processes of state formation and the centralization of government in early modern Europe involved the use of increasing amounts of information. Historians have noted the rise of what the Canadian sociologist Dorothy Smith called 'textually mediated forms of ruling' such as writing letters, writing and annotating reports, issuing forms and questionnaires and so on, associated with what is variously known as the information state, archive state or paper state – now in the process of transforming itself into the digital state.[98] This process may be described as the rise of 'bureaucracy' in the original sense of the term, the rule of the bureau, or office, and its officials. These officials both issued and followed written orders and recorded these orders in their files, together with the reports on the political situation at home and abroad that assisted decision-making. The ruler on horseback was gradually transformed into the ruler sitting at his desk, as in the famous cases of Philip II of Spain in the sixteenth century and Louis XIV of France in the seventeenth.

Information was sometimes collected by means of printed forms (used as early as the sixteenth century in Venice to compile the census) and also by the use of questionnaires, as in the case of the Spanish Empire, where the systematic collection of information about the New World began in 1569, when 37-point questionnaires were sent to local officials in Mexico and Peru, followed in 1577 by a printed 50-point questionnaire. As the German historian Arndt Brendecke has pointed out, empiricism was a tool of empire.[99]

As we have seen, imperial regimes, especially new imperial regimes, have an especially urgent need for information about the lands that form part of their empire. However, since early modern governments were making increasing demands on the population, whether for taxes, military service or religious conformity, they increasingly employed similar methods at home. Jean-Baptiste Colbert, for instance, best-known as Louis XIV's finance minister, might equally well be regarded as a minister of information. For example, he re-established the provincial officials known as intendants, but 'transformed their functions', from tax-collectors into observers and informers, producing 'a massive bank of information'. As Jacob Soll remarks, 'Detail even extended to counting the number of cows in a given locale.' Colbert sent out questionnaires, received reports from India and elsewhere, tried to bring learning under the control of the state and established archives so that the information collected could be preserved and retrieved.[100]

The choice of these European examples does not imply that governments elsewhere did not participate in this general process. In the early modern Mughal Empire, the regime of Akbar was known as 'government by paper' (*kaghazi raj*), a system that was taken over by the East India Company as they began to rule as well as trade. The early modern Chinese government was also a great producer of official paper.[101]

The centralization of government went still further in Europe from the eighteenth century onwards, when the knowledgeable state gradually became more and more of a surveillance state, whether the surveillance was carried out by human informers or, in recent years, by cameras, microphones and computers. Surveillance was assisted by the demand that individuals carry identification papers of some kind. Passports have long existed, but as a general requirement for travel to foreign countries they go back only to the First World War, while the system was codified at conferences organized by the League of Nations in the 1920s. In many countries identity cards became a requirement for all citizens – in France in 1940, in Germany at about the same time, and so on.[102]

Interpretations of the utilization of information by the state are controversial. On one side, presenting what might be called a 'malign interpretation' of the motives of governments, there is Michel Foucault, emphasizing the desire to control. His supporters would include the British historian Vic Gatrell, citing for example the establishment of the British Habitual Criminals Register (1869), which made it easier to put second offenders back into prison. By contrast, another British historian, Edward Higgs, offers a more 'benign' interpretation of the official uses of information. Focusing like Gatrell on the nineteenth century, Higgs argues that information collected by the central government was employed essentially to empower, to defend and diffuse the rights of individuals (to pensions, for example). He suggests that information 'underpins general rights and liberties within a pluralist society'.[103] In early modern times, too, some information had been collected for the purpose of welfare: censuses of mouths to feed in a given city in times of famine, for instance. As is so often the case, each interpretation has something to be said for it, with the relative importance of welfare and surveillance varying with particular regimes.

Employing knowledge in business

Studies of the uses of knowledge in business are multiplying. One focus of interest is the merchant's manual. From the later Middle Ages onwards, more and more manuals were produced to provide merchants, especially merchants living abroad, with essential information about keeping their accounts and about the commodities and the weights and measures and currencies that a Venetian, for instance, would find in Florence, in Bruges, in Aleppo and so on, as well as tips on how to avoid being cheated. A kind of practical knowledge, more or less tacit, which had formerly been transmitted by example or by word of mouth to relatives and employees, was now written down, printed, and so made more widely available.[104]

As enterprises grew larger in the age of trading companies that bought and sold in many parts of the world, their need for written information increased. A famous example of what would now be described as a 'knowledge-creating company' is the Dutch East India Company, founded in 1602 and known as the VOC (*Vereenigde Oost-Indische Compagnie*). The VOC has been described as an early 'multinational' and its remarkable success has sometimes been attributed to the efficiency of its communications network, passing information from the centre in Amsterdam to the Asian headquarters in Batavia (now Jakarta), and the branches in Nagasaki, Surat and elsewhere, and even more important, passing information from the local branches to the centre. The Company's maps and charts were constantly updated as new information was gathered. Bribes, described euphemistically as 'gratuities', gave the company access to information from both Dutch and foreign diplomats. What was most remarkable about the information system of the VOC was the use of regular written reports that provided essential commercial information, often in the form of statistics: reports from local branches and an annual report from the Governor-General in Batavia to the directors in Amsterdam. By the end of the seventeenth century, sales figures were already being analysed in order to determine the future policy of the company on pricing and the ordering of pepper and other commodities from Asia.[105]

What was still unusual in what we might call the 'knowledge policy' of the VOC was to become commonplace later, especially at the time of the rise of large manufacturing firms in the USA and elsewhere in the late nineteenth century. Like states, these firms were bureaucracies, administered by officials known as 'managers'. More and more information came into the firm and circulated through it, in the form of statistics, reports, correspondence, written orders, and so on, assisted by the rise of new office technology, from the typewriter and the filing cabinet to the paper clip.[106] The late nineteenth century was also the time of the rise of what is now known as 'Research and Development' or 'R & D', with large firms constructing laboratories and hiring scientists in order to produce new or improved products. In 1876, for instance, the inventor Thomas Edison opened what has been called the first industrial research laboratory in the world in Menlo Park, New Jersey. Chemists were employed to discover synthetic dyes and pharmacologists to discover new remedies.

There was also increasing concern at this time to circulate information about the firm and its products by means of advertising in newspapers, on posters and on the radio. Thanks to aggressive advertising, 'Pears Soap' had already become household words in late Victorian England. By the 1930s, Americans were being interviewed on the street in order to discover the effectiveness of advertising. Systematic 'market research' had begun.

Re-employment

In the last few pages, the uses of knowledge in the religious, political and economic domains have been discussed separately. However, re-employment should not be forgotten. Both techniques for acquiring information and information itself have sometimes been transferred from one 'employer' to another. In early modern Europe, for instance, the questionnaire, a tool for acquiring useful knowledge, was transferred from the Church to the state. In the United States in the twentieth century, the techniques of market research were adapted to political uses, taking the form of public opinion polls. Changes in the display of artefacts in shop windows were imitated by the curators of museums. Card-indexes spread from offices to libraries and the studies of individual scholars.

Transfers from the political to the academic domain have also taken place. The documents in the archives of government were originally preserved because it was thought that they might be useful in the everyday task of administration. It was only from the French Revolution onwards that government archives were gradually opened to the public, especially though not exclusively to professional historians. The French Archives Nationales were established in 1800; the English Public Record Office opened in 1838; the Spanish archive at Simancas opened in the 1840s; the Vatican Archives opened in 1881, and so on. Following the collapse of the Communist regimes in Europe after 1989, even the files of secret police forces such as the East German Stasi were opened to the public and studies based on this material have begun to appear.

Misemployment

The consequences of employing different kinds of knowledge include some that are unintended and, on occasion, disastrous. As the English poet Alexander Pope memorably wrote, 'A little knowledge is a dangerous thing.' This is the central argument of a book by James Scott, *Seeing Like a State* (1998). An anthropologist who has carried out fieldwork in South-East Asia and takes a special interest in the problems of peasants, Scott shows 'how certain schemes to improve the human condition have failed'. From the eighteenth century onwards, so he suggests, there have been a succession of attempts 'to make a society legible'. To make it legible means not only to collect maps, statistics and other kinds of information, but also 'to arrange the population in ways that simplified the classic state functions of taxation, conscription and the prevention of rebellion'. Scott begins his account with forestry in Germany, where the state saw forests as sources of revenue, and scientific forestry was concerned with estimating and managing this revenue. 'The German forest became the archetype for imposing on disorderly nature the neatly arranged constructs of science.' The trees were planted in straight rows, as if on parade. From the arrangement of trees, the book moves on to the arrangement of people, discussing what the author calls 'authoritarian High Modernism' via concrete examples such as the collectivization of agriculture in the USSR, the foundation of Brasília, 'compulsory villagization' (in Tanzania), and so on. In each case Scott emphasizes the negative consequences of plans backed by state power and imposed without regard to local conditions and problems.

Seeing Like a State might be described as an anthropologist's critique not only of the modern state but also of sociology and more generally of supposedly universal or context-free knowledge. The author argues that 'certain forms of knowledge and control require a narrowing of vision', and makes an eloquent plea for the valorization of an alternative

knowledge, variously described as local, practical and con-
textualized, 'the valuable knowledge that high-modernist
schemes deprive themselves of when they simply impose their
plans'. More recent studies of the dangers of planning without
local knowledge support Scott's argument.[107]

4
Problems and Prospects

Problems

Studies of the history of knowledge should not be imagined
as so many productions of a scholarly consensus. There are
of course many areas of agreement, but there are also areas
of conflict. An obvious example, discussed in Chapter 2, is
the question of 'orientalism', raised by Edward Said and
taken up by both supporters and critics of his central argument. As in the case of history in general, it is impossible to
study the history of knowledge without encountering problems; old problems such as internal versus external approaches,
change versus continuity, anachronism and relativism, and
newer ones such as triumphalism and constructivism. The
purpose of this chapter is not to offer simple solutions to
complex problems, but to encourage awareness of the decisions, often implicit, that underlie different studies in this
field.

Internal versus external histories

A problem that has already surfaced more than once in this
book is the problem of the relation between knowledge and
society, a problem posed by Marx and Mannheim and
debated ever since. One form that it takes is that of choice

between two approaches to the history of knowledge. On one side, we find the 'internal' approach that explains change in an order of knowledge in terms of growth or decline from within; on the other side, the 'external' approach that links change within a knowledge order to change in the world outside it. In the case of the history of knowledge, one approach would explain the fragmentation of knowledge by the accumulation of information, while the other would view it as part of the increasing division of labour. 'Internalists' find the external approach insensitive, while 'externalists' consider that the internal approach is too narrow.

In this case the problem might be resolved by suggesting that both approaches are necessary, that it is possible, indeed necessary to reconcile them, difficult as this reconciliation may be in practice. On the other hand, other forms of the knowledge and society problem cannot be dismissed so easily. The big question is whether the shape of a given society determines or simply influences the knowledges to be found in it. This question raises a number of others in its turn. What counts as a 'society'? For example, is Britain in the early twenty-first century one society or many? Does 'society' mean the social structure, the division into genders, classes and occupations, or does it include the economic and political systems as well? In the wake of the second wave of the sociology of knowledge, we also need to ask whether it is 'culture' (including fundamental values) rather than society that shapes knowledge in a particular place and time. There is no simple answer to any of these questions, but it would be unwise, to say the least, to embark upon a history of knowledge without bearing them in mind.

Continuities versus revolutions

As in history in general, the relative importance of change and continuity in the history of knowledge continues to provoke debate. It is easy to say that the truth lies between the two extremes, but more difficult to be specific and to differentiate between places, periods and domains. A classic discussion of the problem in the history of science is Thomas Kuhn's *Structure of Scientific Revolutions* (1962).[1] Writing against what he called 'the concept of development-by-accumulation' underlying most earlier histories of science, Thomas Kuhn argued instead for the importance of recurrent revolutions. Each revolution, so he argued, goes through a series of stages. The first stage is the awareness of 'anomaly', in other words the recognition that some information is inconsistent with currently accepted interpretations of the natural world, interpretations that Kuhn described as the 'paradigms' or models of 'normal science' in a given place and time. The second stage is that of the 'crisis' of the paradigm, as anomalies accumulate. The third stage is the 'revolution', in other words the breakthrough to a new paradigm, which when accepted becomes a new form of normal science, to be challenged in its turn by further anomalies.

In France, a critique of the assumption of continuity had been launched a generation earlier than Kuhn by the philosopher Gaston Bachelard. Bachelard, together with Georges Canguilhem, his successor as director of an institute for the history of science in Paris, opposed the idea of the gradual, continuous, cumulative evolution of science, replacing it with the idea of breaks or 'ruptures'. A break was a break-through, the removal of what Bachelard called an 'epistemological obstacle', such as the assumption that things were animate.[2]

Following (paradoxically enough) the tradition established by Bachelard and Canguilhem, Michel Foucault also criticized the emphasis on continuity in histories of knowledge. In its place he advocated what he called an 'archaeology of knowledge', penetrating below the surface, excavating intellectual strata and emphasizing the sharp breaks in different periods between what he called 'discourses' or more generally the 'episteme'.[3] Like Kuhn, Foucault thought in terms of revolution rather than evolution (hence his use of the metaphor of 'birth', as in the case of his book *The Birth of the Clinic*).

In this debate over the relative importance of evolution and revolution, which party has won? There is of course no reason to believe that all change in orders of knowledge or in academic disciplines is of the same type. All the same, it is worth adding that when they are examined in more and more concrete detail, some intellectual revolutions have come to appear less and less revolutionary, notably the famous scientific revolution of the seventeenth century. The American historian Steven Shapin began his book on the subject with the sentence 'There was no such thing as the Scientific Revolution, and this is a book about it', going on to question the existence of 'a coherent, cataclysmic and climactic event that fundamentally and irrevocably changed what people knew about the natural world and how they secured proper knowledge of that world', replacing it with the idea of a plurality of events spread over generations.[4]

A similar point might be made about the nineteenth-century 'revolution' in historical thought associated with Leopold von Ranke. Some historians, following Thomas Kuhn, have written about Ranke's establishment of a new historical 'paradigm'.[5] Ranke was indeed a great historian and one who made a great impact on what was becoming a profession, first in Germany and then elsewhere. His critique of earlier historians, for overemphasizing literary sources such as chronicles and paying insufficient attention to the documents to be found in national and other archives, scored some palpable hits. All the same, Ranke was far from the first historian to work in archives and, ironically enough, the archival sources he is best known for exploiting, the reports of Venetian ambassadors, originally addressed to the Senate of the Republic, were not 'pure' documents but literary productions following rhetorical conventions. Once again, what looks from a distance like a sudden revolution appears in close-up to be part of a more gradual process.

If the close examination of revolutions in knowledge reveals continuities, the reverse is also the case, as a number of studies of tradition, some of them already discussed in Chapter 2, suggest. Although the Latin word *traditio* literally means what is handed down, it would be a mistake, as many scholars have pointed out, to imagine that what is passed from one generation to another remains unchanged. Since the world is always on the move, it can even be argued that if a tradition remained the same it would be different, because its context had altered. For this reason, the Dutch Indologist Jan Heesterman wrote about what he called 'the inner conflict of traditions'. Hence the need to reconstruct them, or even to invent new ones, as well as the attempt to disguise change by claiming that a given institution was, as the

Catholic Church asserted at the time of the Reformation, *semper eadem* ('always the same').[6]

Anachronism

One consequence of disguising change within tradition is to encourage anachronistic interpretations of the past. Among historians, anachronism is generally considered a mortal sin, perhaps the mortal sin *par excellence*, since it signifies unawareness of change, the historian's speciality.

All the same, some distinguished historians deliberately employ anachronistic phrases. Their point, whether explicit or implicit, is that historians are translators from the culture of the past into that of the present, and that like translators between languages they face the difficult choice between fidelity to the culture they are translating from and intelligibility to the culture they are translating into. If they place the emphasis on fidelity, translators adopt the strategy of 'foreignization', leaving technical terms in the original language, writing about seventeenth-century 'natural philosophy' rather than 'science', Chinese *shen-shi* rather than 'scholar-gentry', Ottoman *medreses* or Arab *madrasas* rather than 'mosque schools', German *Bildung* rather than 'general education' and so on.[7]

On the other hand, if they place the emphasis on intelligibility, translators choose the strategy of 'domestication', using familiar modern Western terms such as 'university', 'science' and so on to refer to institutions or practices in places or periods in which these concepts did not exist, although knowledge was transmitted and nature was investigated. Domestication brings the reader closer to the past, at the price of possible confusions between past and present, while foreignization preserves the uniqueness of past cultures at the price of making them seem remote.

As a case-study of the problem we might take the concept of the 'intellectual'. As we saw in Chapter 2, the term came into use in France at the end of the nineteenth century in the context of the notorious 'Dreyfus Affair'. This moment, in which some writers, scientists and scholars participated in a public debate, has been described as the moment of 'the birth of the intellectual'. The term *intellectuel* was indeed coined in French at this time and soon spread to other languages such as Italian, Spanish and English.[8] Strictly speaking, then, it is anachronistic to use the term 'intellectual' to refer to knowledgeable people living in a period before it was coined, although it is difficult not to think of Voltaire in this way, since he was not only what his contemporaries called a 'man of letters' but also an individual as deeply involved in public, political controversies as (say) Zola in the nineteenth century or Sartre in the twentieth.

Some leading historians would go further in this direction. In a characteristically bold essay, published early in his long career, the great French medievalist Jacques Le Goff presented the scholastic philosophers of the twelfth and thirteen centuries, known at the time as *philosophi* or *magistri*, as 'intellectuals'. A more recent study of this intellectual world by Jacques Verger, although respectful to Le Goff, prefers what the author calls the more 'neutral' modern phrase, *gens de savoir* ('knowledgeable people'). On the other hand, some contributors to a recent collection of essays on early medieval 'lay intellectuals' defend their use of the term on the grounds that their concern is with scholars who – like Zola or Sartre – were involved in public debates.[9]

It is certainly convenient to have a general term that facilitates comparisons between the Chinese *shen-shi*, the *'ulema* of the Muslim world (above, Chapter 1), Indian *pandits*, the Russian *intelligentsia* and so on. The problem is that the use of a general term irons out differences between the social role of knowledgeable people in these different cultures. The practice of alternation between the general term and the specific ones offers a pragmatic solution, but the problem of what is lost in translation remains. Behind it looms a still greater problem, that of the 'commensurability' or 'incommensurability' of concepts.[10] This in turn raises the spectre of relativism.

Relativism

It is impossible to go very far in the study of knowledge, whether in space, time or indeed within a given society, without encountering a variety of traditions. Confronted with this variety, historians face a difficult choice, whether to assert (or at least to assume) the superiority of a single tradition, usually the Western scientific tradition, thus incurring the charge of ethnocentrism, or to treat all claims to knowledge as equal, incurring the charge of relativism or even nihilism. Since a number of scholars studying what they call knowledges in the plural have recently opted for the second strategy, this section focuses on the problems raised by that choice.

Karl Mannheim's famous discussion of situated knowledge, discussed earlier, implied a kind of relativism, although Mannheim himself distinguished what he called 'relationism', emphasizing the way in which beliefs are 'bound' to a particular place, time and social group, from what he called 'a philosophical relativism' that denies the validity of any distinction between truth and falsehood. This distinction has incurred some criticism.[11]

On the other side, Mannheim has been criticized, notably by the sociologist of science David Bloor, for a failure of nerve in exempting the natural sciences from his account of situated knowledge. Ludwik Fleck, whose work was discussed in Chapter 2, had already made the same criticism of Durkheim, another believer in what has been called the 'sociological immunity' of science. Thomas Kuhn responded to the challenge by arguing that different scientific theories are the product of what he called 'incommensurable ways of seeing the world', while Bloor himself put forward what he called a 'strong programme' in the sociology of science, arguing that for sociologists knowledge is whatever is taken to be knowledge in a given milieu or culture.[12]

Anthropologists too usually take this position, linked to the idea of the incommensurablity not of theories but of whole cultures. As Fredrik Barth puts it, 'We want to be able to ... exercise the relativism whereby all of the traditions, bodies of knowledge and ways of knowing practiced by people are recognized for our comparative and analytic purposes as coeval and sustainable, each on its own premises.'[13] As we have seen, some anthropologists, putting the denial of 'sociological immunity' into practice, have carried out 'fieldwork' in laboratories, for instance, in order to observe modern Western scientific knowledge in the making.[14] In complementary fashion, other anthropologists place Western science and ethno-science (otherwise known as 'indigenous knowledge') on the same footing in order to view what they call 'a more naked science', emphasizing similarities rather than differences between 'Us' and 'Them'.[15]

At this point it may be useful to distinguish the philosopher's problem of relativism from that of the historian. Philosophers continue to disagree about the way to solve the problem of relativism, or better, relativisms in the plural – moral, cognitive, subjective and so on. For historians, on the other hand, the pressing problem is a pragmatic one. To understand past knowledge systems it is not necessary to assert that they are equally effective in understanding the world. On the other hand, we do need to treat them on equal terms. Attitudes that appear to us to be naive or credulous – the belief in the efficacy of witchcraft, for instance – should not be judged by our standards but related to the culture of which they formed a part, the local norms, including the standards of verification current in a given place and time. Documents that appear to be inaccurate, like the Inuit maps discussed in Chapter 3, may simply reveal a different understanding of space from our own. The essential point is to take seriously the knowledges and the intellectual categories of other cultures, rather than viewing them from a position of superiority as so many errors or 'superstitions'.

Triumphalism

The history of knowledge is often written as the history of success, of ever-increasing information, knowledge and understanding. There have certainly been many triumphs, most obviously the discoveries and theories associated with Copernicus, Newton, Darwin, Einstein and other scientists, or in the humanities the more gradual development of textual criticism, comparative linguistics, the decoding of dead languages and so on. More generally, it has been argued that the history of humanity is the history of 'collective learning' in which knowledge has accumulated and has been shared more and more widely as different groups and cultures have encountered one another.[16]

On the other hand, we should remember that knowledge can be lost as well as gained, if knowledgeable people die without passing on what they have learned or if archives and libraries go up in flames. The burning of the library of Alexandria, the greatest library of classical antiquity, offers a notorious example of this process, like the 'burning of books and burial of scholars' in 213 BCE by order of the first emperor of China, Qin Shi Huang.

In some places and at some moments, such as the decline of the Roman Empire at the time of the invasions of the so-called 'barbarians', a great deal of what had been known in the ancient world was lost as a result of the devaluation of 'pagan' knowledge in the Christian world as well as the decline or destruction of its former centres. Among the losses was the knowledge of Greek, and with it other kinds of knowledge, including medical knowledge.[17]

Although knowledge, or even learning, is not confined to books, the small numbers of texts in circulation in early medieval Europe are likely to shock modern readers. We need to imagine a world in which a relatively large library contained only four hundred books or even fewer. In the eighth century, the historian Bede, who worked in a monastery in Northumbria, was privileged, since he had access to more than three hundred books. In the ninth century, the library of the monastery of Reichenau contained 415 books, and that of St Gall, 395. In his famous study of the Middle Ages, Richard Southern tells the story of the correspondence between Raginbold of Cologne and Radolf of Liège, c.1025, in which they discussed the ideas of the late classical scholar Boethius but were unable to understand what he meant by the 'interior angles' of a triangle, 'a forcible reminder', as Southern says, 'of the vast scientific ignorance with which the age was faced'.[18]

Collectively, we now know much more than Raginbold and Radolf, indeed more than Boethius and Aristotle. However, this increase comes at a price. Some scholars speak of 'information overload', in other words the accumulation of 'raw' data faster than it can be processed and turned into knowledge. Overload was already the subject of complaint in the sixteenth century, soon after the spread of printed books.[19] The problem has become increasingly acute in our time, with the 'explosion' of information discussed earlier.

In any case, even if humanity as a whole knows more today than at any time in the past, we cannot say the same about individual humans. Our memories have not improved and we do not study for longer hours than our predecessors, so that if we know some things that they did not, the reverse is also the case. Consequently, histories of knowledge need to include ignorance, obstacles to knowledge and conflicts between knowledges, sometimes ending in the collective rejection of what had been believed to be knowledge, as in the cases of alchemy, phrenology and so on.[20]

Constructivism

Historians, like scientists, long viewed knowledge of the world as 'an assemblage of accurate representations'.[21] As in the case of the gradual accumulation of knowledge, discussed above, this view was opposed by Bachelard, Kuhn and Foucault. Bachelard, for instance, claimed that 'Nothing is given. Everything is constructed.' This position has come to be described as 'constructivist epistemology', with the construction sometimes qualified as either social or cultural. It is part of the trend that the French historian Roger Chartier has described as the shift 'from the social history of culture to the cultural history of society'.[22]

As has often been the case in histories of knowledge, it is the scholars working on the history of the natural sciences who first exemplified this shift from what Jan Golinski has called a view of scientific knowledge as 'the revelation of a pre-given order of nature' to a view of it as 'a human product made with locally situated cultural and material resources'. Golinski focuses on the problem of moving from experiments conducted by particular people in particular places, 'the local culture of physics laboratories' for instance, to scientific laws of supposedly general validity. The paradox of universal knowledge being produced in specific environments has inspired recent studies in the geography of knowledge, examining regions, networks, botanical gardens and so on.[23]

In the social sciences, Pierre Bourdieu emphasized the way in which the social position of sociologists affects their perception of the societies that they study.[24] In the humanities too the 'constructivists', as it is convenient to call them, have drawn attention to the active role of discoverers (whether they are conscious of this or not) in the creation of the phenomena that they believe they have discovered. They impose categories on what they observe and on occasion at least, especially when the discoverers are in a position of power, these categories come to seem natural, even among the people observed.

Again, scholars often find what they expect or want to find or view the social world through the tinted spectacles of intellectual paradigms, not to mention less sophisticated stereotypes such as (for Westerners) the passive or lazy 'oriental'. Western historians, for example, familiar with the idea of the feudal system, 'discovered' feudalism in India and Japan, impressed as they were by specific similarities and passing over the important differences between these regimes.

Constructivism was encouraged, indeed it was put on the intellectual map, by two ethnographies of scientists at work, *Laboratory Life* (1979) by Bruno Latour and Stephen Woolgar, subtitled 'the construction of scientific facts', and *The Manufacture of Knowledge* (1981) by Karin Knorr-Cetina. For a time, especially in the 1980s and 1990s, the term 'invention' became a favourite term in the titles of books, as in the case of studies of the invention of Africa, Spain, Scotland and, most memorable for historians, *The Invention of Tradition*.[25]

The reaction against simplistic assumptions of 'discovery' and 'objectivity' was a salutary one, but – as is often the case in the history of scholarship – the pendulum swung from one extreme to another. Today, it seems to have settled somewhere in the middle. This middle position has much to be said for it. Invention out of nothing is as implausible as a simple uncovering of what was always there. Taking the term 'construction' somewhat more literally than many of its users have done, we might pay attention to the raw materials used in the building. We might also speak and think in terms of 'reconstruction'.

Returning to the example of the British in India, discussed in Chapter 2, they neither discovered nor invented the caste system, but they reconstructed it. As Nicholas Dirks suggests, 'caste, as we know it today, is not some unchanged survival of ancient India', but 'the product of an historical encounter between India and Western colonial rule'.[26] The British may have misinterpreted the Indian social system, but they had the power to make their misinterpretation become the new reality. Something similar may have occurred in England after 1066, when the Norman conquerors, uninterested in the more complex social distinctions to be found in Anglo-Saxon society, imposed a simple division between free peasants and serfs.

Agents versus systems

In historical writing as in sociology and anthropology there has been a long debate over the relative importance of social structures or systems and that of individual agents, or actors. The history of knowledge is no exception here.

On one side, Fredrik Barth's anthropology of knowledge emphasizes agency, 'the knowers' and 'the acts of the knowers' – the people who hold, learn, produce and apply knowledge in their various activities and lives. On the other, Bourdieu's *Homo academicus*, discussed in an earlier chapter, sustained with his usual brilliance an argument for the primacy of what we referred to in Chapter 2 as 'orders of knowledge', or as Bourdieu preferred to say, of positions in the academic 'field' and the inheritance of cultural capital.[27]

All the same, it might be argued that the career of Bourdieu himself, the son of a rural postman in the Southwest who became a professor at the Collège de France in Paris, suggests the possibility of exceptions to his rules. As in the case of other dichotomies discussed in this chapter, a position somewhere in the middle is to be recommended, as a vantage point from which to view both the insights and the limitations of the two opposites.

From a social point of view, a system of knowledge includes the roles available for individuals to perform, the criteria for a good performance, and the way in which different kinds of knowledge are transmitted. It may be imagined as a network of opportunities and constraints, opportunities and constraints that are not always visible to the agents. Although this proposition would not be easy to test, it might be argued that successful agents in a given culture of knowledge are the ones whose abilities best fit the system. On the other hand, different systems offer more or less space for individual agents to do things their own way, just as they offer more or less space for innovation.

Take the case, or more exactly the different cases (since the regime in Poland, for instance, was less rigid than that of East Germany), of the academic systems in the Communist states of East-Central and Eastern Europe in the age of the Cold War. The constraints of the 'party line' were obvious enough to both insiders and outsiders. All the same, some creative individual academics were able not only to survive in the system, in spite of the obstacles to the careers of non-conformists, but also to produce work that won them respect in other countries, not only in the natural sciences, where there was less political interference with research, but in the humanities as well. In the USSR, for instance, the literary theorist Mikhail Bakhtin, the folklorist Vladimir Propp, the semiologist Yuri Lotman and the historian Aron Gurevich were all able to publish work of lasting value, recognized both unofficially at home and in public abroad. Even systems of knowledge that appear to outsiders to offer agents no room to manoeuvre have such spaces, just as systems that appear to offer great freedom may include constraints.

Gender

It may seem odd to be discussing gender here, since the relative roles of men and women in the history of knowledge might be better regarded as a topic than as a problem. However, the topic certainly raises problems, beginning with the fact that little attention was paid to the place of women in the story until quite recently. This inattention may be explained by the dominance of men in the historical profession as well as by the relative 'invisibility' of women in the past.

The history of gendered knowledges illustrates some of the themes discussed in the preceding section on system and agency, since for a long time the dominant order of knowledge had little room for females. Women were generally excluded from formal institutions of knowledge such as universities or learned societies until the late nineteenth century. Obstacles to their progress remained, but careers of individuals such as the physicist Marie Skłodowska-Curie, psychoanalysts such as Melanie Klein, and classicists such as Jane Harrison became possible.

Before 1800, women were active in roles such as 'midwife' and 'wise woman', but oral transmission imposed 'a strict limit to pass on the knowledge that any woman or group of women might accumulate over a lifetime of practice'. From an academic point of view, female expertise did not count as knowledge, and it was increasingly challenged by males. In the case of midwives this challenge was already visible as early as the fifteenth century, when physicians such as Michele Savonarola began to treat infertility, to supervise pregnancy and childbirth and to give advice about the health of small children.[28] Following the model of Virginia Woolf's famous essay on 'Shakespeare's sister', one might imagine the career – or non-career – of Newton's sister, as intelligent and curious as he was but lacking his opportunities.

However, women did have a certain room for manoeuvre, especially behind the scenes. Before 1800, exceptional European women travelled the world and searched for knowledge, like the German naturalist Maria Sibylla Merian in eighteenth-century Surinam, who took more interest than her male colleagues in plants that assisted contraception and abortion, obtaining the information about them from female slaves.[29] However, it was only in the later twentieth century that such activity behind the scenes began to be taken seriously by social historians.

As we saw in Chapter 1, the new wave of feminism in the 1970s made an impact on the sociology of knowledge. Situated knowledge, viewed earlier mainly in terms of social class, was discussed by Donna Haraway and others in terms of gender.[30] More recently, a series of studies, mainly by female scholars, has drawn attention to contributions to knowledge made by women in a number of different domains, places and periods. Some studies focus on the obstacles in the way of women who wanted to become scholars, in the manner of Germaine Greer's study of female painters, *The Obstacle Race* (1979), while others emphasize the positive contributions that certain women were able to make.

Both these points are vividly illustrated in Ann Shteir's study of women as botanists in nineteenth-century England. The collection of plants, especially flowers, was considered a ladylike pursuit. So was painting them and writing about them, especially writing for children. As long as botany formed part of a general natural history, the participation of female amateurs posed no problem. After 1830, however, as botanical culture became more professional and more scientific, in other words an academic discipline, the subject was 'defeminized'. Even women who contributed to the new science were marginalized. Agnes Ibbetson, for instance, published articles on plant physiology and was not afraid to criticize the work of fellow-botanists, but she received only a 'poor response' from male colleagues.[31]

The writing of history itself has been examined from these points of view, notably by Bonnie Smith, proposing that 'the development of modern scientific methodology, epistemology, professional practice and writing has been closely tied to evolving definitions of masculinity and femininity'.[32] Smith distinguishes three main groups of female historians: first the amateurs, such as the sisters Agnes and Elizabeth Strickland, joint authors of lives of the queens of England, or Julia Cartwright, the biographer of the 'Renaissance woman' Isabella d' Este; secondly, the assistants, carrying out research for more famous male historians, as Lucie Varga did for Lucien Febvre, or writing books jointly with them but receiving less of the credit, as in the case of Mary Beard's contribution to *The Rise of American Civilization* (1927), written with her husband Charles; and in the third place, the professionals, often paid less or waiting longer for promotion than their male colleagues, but including scholars of the distinction of the medievalist Eileen Power, one of the first women to become a professor at the London School of Economics (in 1931). Power was the author of *Medieval People* (1924) and *Medieval Women* (1975: it is surely significant that this book had to wait so long to be published, thirty-five years after the death of its author).

From the perspective of 'women's ways of knowing', discussed in Chapter 1, it may also be significant that the contribution of female historians has been especially important in economic history and the history of everyday life; witness not only Power's books but also Alice Clark's pioneering *Working Life of Women in the Seventeenth Century* (1919) and the work of Lucy Salmon, professor at Vassar College in the USA from 1889 to 1927, who, as Smith says, 'taught the uses of a virtually unlimited, even low kind of source material. Railroad schedules, laundry lists, trash piles, kitchen appliances, the position of trees and the condition of buildings in urban spaces conveyed critical historical information'.[33]

Prospects

Turning now to the 'foreseeable future' – in other words the near future, whether foreseeable or not – I believe that we shall see increasing emphasis on the place of knowledge in other kinds of history. A move in this direction has certainly been made by economic historians such as David Landes, who wrote an economic history of the rise of the West that explained this rise essentially as a result of 'the gains from the application of knowledge and science to technology'. Again and again in his narrative, Landes stressed what he called 'the accumulation of knowledge and knowhow' and the importance of learning from competitors, as the nineteenth-century Japanese did while the French did not.[34]

Again, in the case of military history, Peter Paret has discussed what he calls the 'cognitive challenge' of warfare, noting how Carl von Clausewitz developed his theory of war in response to Napoleon's defeat of Prussia in 1806.[35] On the other hand, historians of political thought have so far said relatively little about the political knowledge that supported both the generalizations and the recommendations of the writers that they study, even though some political thinkers, such as Aristotle or Jean Bodin, took care to gather large quantities of information about a variety of political regimes, while others, such as Niccolò Machiavelli, drew on the experience of a life in politics.

Within the history of knowledges themselves, I believe that three approaches will become increasingly important in the coming decades: a global approach, a social approach and a concern with the very long run.

In the first place, as in the case of history in general, we can already see a global turn, going beyond studies of particular parts of the world such as India or China and organized not around the diffusion of Western knowledge or even around colonialism, much studied recently, but around encounters, clashes, translations and hybridizations. Some recent studies have concentrated on 'knowledge on the move', often over long distances.[36] As has so often happened in the history of knowledge, historians of the natural sciences have led the way, though scholars working on the history of historical thought and writing have been moving in the same direction.[37] Comparisons between cultures distant from one another, such as ancient Greece and ancient China, are making their contribution to this trend.

In the second place, we can see a social turn, including a history of knowledge from below, examining, for instance, the employment of information not only by governments but also by the governed, whether to vote in a particular way, to organize protests or even to make revolutions. Another aspect of the social approach, once again an extension of a tendency already visible in the present, is an increasing interest in everyday knowledges, including the tacit, bodily knowledges discussed in Chapter 2, not only in crafts such as metalworking but also in fields as diverse as diplomacy, trade, connoisseurship, management and sport. In the last case, exemplary studies of boxing and *capoeira*, written by anthropologists whose fieldwork included training in these arts, deserve to inspire historians.[38] The role of the coach in making tacit knowledge explicit might make an illuminating topic for future investigation.

In the third place, in the near future we are likely to see more emphasis on collective learning on the part of humanity over the very long term, attempting to answer the big question posed by one of the protagonists of Big History, 'How did this pooling and sharing of knowledge generate the

long-term changes that distinguish the history of humans
from that of closely related species?'[39] The challenge is to fill
in the outline offered by David Christian, who has noted, for
instance, that increasing dense settlement 'encouraged more
exchanges of ideas' as agriculture developed.[40] The response
to this challenge might be described as 'cognitive history'.
Cognitive history may appear to be the history of collective
mentalities under another name, but it is concerned with a
period much longer than the *longue durée* of the French
Annales School, with millennia rather than centuries. To go
further in this direction, historians will need the help of
archaeologists, in other words an 'archaeology of knowledge'
in the literal rather than the Foucauldian sense. Archaeologists have long been interested in the reconstruction of
knowledge in 'prehistoric' times, in other words before the
invention of writing systems, using the evidence of material
remains. They concern themselves with the turning-points
when humans began to use language, to make paintings and
carvings, or to bury their dead in elaborate graves. In their
attempts to reconstruct prehistoric worlds of knowledge and
ways of thought, archaeologists began by a kind of intellectual subtraction, 'draining off' later knowledges.[41]

As we saw in Chapter 1, later archaeologists turned
towards anthropology, since many anthropologists have
studied small-scale societies with simple technologies, while
some of them have turned to cognitive science to help them
study what they call 'embodied cognition'. In similar fashion,
archaeologists have made use of the findings of cognitive
science in the search for the 'ancient mind', practising a 'cognitive archaeology' of the kind advocated by Colin Renfrew
and others.[42] Studies of later periods are fewer, although an
attempt has recently been made to draw on cognitive studies
for a history of remembering in early modern England,
focused on religion and education.[43]

Whether future historians of knowledge will draw on cognitive science or neuroscience is a more difficult question. For
'Big' or 'Deep' historians, concerned with a hundred thousand years or more, the idea of 'cognitive evolution' makes
obvious sense. 'Evolution' in the Darwinian sense of the term,
in other words the enlargement of brains and the growth of
cognitive abilities by natural selection, is the red thread in

the long and complex story running from the apes to *Homo habilis* (already using tools 2.7 million years ago), *Homo erectus* (standing upright) and finally to *Homo sapiens*.[44]

More problematic is the relevance of cognitive studies to the study of the history of the last five thousand years or so, on which most historians concentrate their attention. Even here, though, a fruitful intellectual exchange may be possible. In the case of the history of knowledge, the recent convergence between the conclusions of cognitive psychologists and oral historians who study memory is worth noting. After the space shuttle *Challenger* exploded in 1986, for instance, a psychologist conducted an experiment, twice asking the same group of people what they remembered about the incident, on the first occasion on the day after the accident and a second time three years later. He looked for discrepancies between the two accounts in order to show the unreliability of memory.[45]

Oral historians have also interviewed the same witnesses more than once and learned both how and how much their memories changed over time. Each group of researchers might learn something from the other. The psychologists are better at explaining why our memories change over time, while the historians are better at explaining how they change, emphasizing what might be called the 'mythologization' of memory, the contamination of memories of personal experiences by the stories current in a given culture. For example, the memories of Australian soldiers who fought in the First World War were influenced by their memories of films or television serials representing the same events.[46]

Historians like to point out that if anything is certain about the future, it is that it will differ from all the predictions made about it. All the same, whatever the new trends in the history of knowledge will be in the coming decades, it is likely that interest in the subject by members of our 'knowledge society' will continue to grow.

Notes

1 Knowledges and their Histories

1 P. Drucker, *Post-Capitalist Society*, Oxford 1993, 30.
2 R. D. Brown, *Knowledge is Power: The Diffusion of Information in Early America, 1700–1865*, New York 1989; F. K. Ringer, *Fields of Knowledge: French Academic Culture in Comparative Perspective, 1890–1920*, Cambridge 1992; B. S. Cohn, *Colonialism and its Forms of Knowledge*, Princeton NJ 1996.
3 M. Daunton (ed.) *The Organisation of Knowledge in Victorian Britain*, Oxford 2005.
4 C. Jacob (ed.) *Lieux de Savoir*, 2 vols., Paris 2007–11.
5 P. Sarrasin, 'Was ist Wissensgeschichte?' *Internationales Archiv für Sozialgeschichte der deutschen Literatur* 26 (2011), presents a manifesto for the approach of the centre.
6 P. K. O'Brien, 'Historical foundations for a global perspective on the emergence of a West European regime for the discovery, development and diffusion of useful and reliable knowledge', *Journal of Global History* 8 (2013), 1–24.
7 F. Bacon, *Advancement of Learning* (1605: new edn, London 1915), 62, 70.
8 M. C. Carhart, '*Historia Literaria* and the science of culture from Mylaeus to Eichhorn', in P. N. Miller (ed.) *Momigliano and Antiquarianism*, Toronto 2007, 184–206.
9 K. Mannheim, 'The problem of a sociology of knowledge' (1925), English trans. in his *Essays in the Sociology of Knowledge*, London 1952, 134–90; R. K. Merton, 'The sociology of

knowledge' (1945), rpr. his *Social Theory and Social Structure,* 2nd edn Glencoe IL 1957, 456–88.

10 U. J. Schneider, 'Wissensgeschichte, nicht Wissenschaftsgeschichte', in A. Honneth and M. Saar (eds.) *Michel Foucault: Zwischenbalanz einer Rezeption,* Frankfurt 2003, 220–9; J. Vogel, 'Von der Wissenschafts- zur Wissengeschichte', *Geschichte und Gesellschaft* 30 (2004), 639–60; Sarrasin, 'Was ist Wissensgeschichte?'.

11 F. Machlup, *The Production and Distribution of Knowledge in the United States,* Princeton NJ 1962; D. Bell, *The Coming of Post-Industrial Society,* London 1974.

12 Vogel, 'Von der Wissenschafts- zur Wissensgeschichte'; R. van Dülmen and S. Rauschenbach (eds.) *Macht des Wissens. Die Entstehung der modernen Wissensgesellschaft,* Cologne 2004.

13 R. Darnton, 'An early information society: News and the media in eighteenth-century Paris, *American Historical Review* 105 (2000), 1–35; A. D. Chandler and J. W. Cortada (eds.) *A Nation Transformed by Information,* New York 2000.

14 J. Raven, *What is the History of the Book?* Cambridge, forthcoming.

15 H. Plotkin, *The Nature of Knowledge,* Cambridge MA 1994; cf. N. Stehr and R. Grundmann, *Knowledge: Critical Concepts,* 4 vols., London 2005.

16 Chandler and Cortada, note 13 above; D. R. Headrick, *When Information came of Age: Technologies of Knowledge in the Age of Reason and Revolution, 1700–1850,* New York 2001.

17 Drucker, *Post-Capitalist Society;* P. Worsley, *Knowledges: What Different Peoples Make of the World,* London 2007, 10.

18 P. Dear, *Revolutionizing the Sciences: European Knowledge and its Ambitions, 1500–1700,* Basingstoke 2001, 10–29, 168–70.

19 W. Detel and C. Zittel, 'Ideals and cultures of knowledge in early modern Europe', in Detel and Zittel (eds.) *Wissensideale und Wissenskulturen in der frühen Neuzeit,* Berlin 2002, 7–22.

20 M. Mulsow, *Präkares Wissen: eine andere Ideengeschichte der Frühen Neuzeit,* Frankfurt 2012.

21 F. Rosenthal, *Knowledge Triumphant,* Leiden 1970; A. H. Hourani, *A History of the Arab Peoples,* London 1991, 158–71.

22 J. Ackerman, ' "Ars sine scientia nihil est": Gothic theory of architecture at the cathedral of Milan', *Art Bulletin* 12 (1949), 84–108; J. Henry, 'Doctors and healers: Popular culture and the medical profession', in S. Pumfrey, P. Rossi and M. Slawinski (eds.) *Science, Culture and Popular Belief in Renaissance*

Europe, Manchester 1991, 191–221; S. L. Kaplan, *Provisioning Paris*, Ithaca NY 1984, 457–63.

23   L. Daston and E. Lunbeck, *Histories of Scientific Observation*, Chicago IL 2011; L. Daston and P. Galison, *Objectivity*, New York 2011; T. Curnow, *Wisdom: A History*, London 2015.

24   T. Becher, *Academic Tribes and Territories: Intellectual Enquiry and the Cultures of Disciplines*, Milton Keynes 1989.

25   M. Foucault, *Power/Knowledge: Selected Interviews and Other Writings, 1972–1977*, Brighton 1980, 52.

26   Bacon, *Advancement of Learning*, 10, 70.

27   K. Mannheim, *Ideology and Utopia* (1929), English trans. London 1936, 239, 244, 247–8.

28   A. Swidler and J. Arditi, 'The new sociology of knowledge', *Annual Review of Sociology* 20 (1994), 305–29; E. D. McCarthy, *Knowledge as Culture: The New Sociology of Knowledge*, London 1996.

29   Mannheim, *Ideology and Utopia*, 69; P. Bourdieu, *Homo Academicus* (194), English trans. Stanford 1988; *Science of Science and Reflexivity* (2001), English trans. Cambridge 2004.

30   D. Bloor, *Knowledge and Social Imagery*, London 1976.

31   D. Haraway, 'Situated knowledge', *Feminist Studies* 14 (1988), 575–99; L. Schiebinger, *The Mind has no Sex? Women in the Origins of Modern Science*. Cambridge MA 1989; M. F. Belenky et al., *Women's Ways of Knowing*, New York 1976; D. E. Smith, *The Conceptual Practices of Power: A Feminist Sociology of Knowledge*. Boston 1990; L. Alcoff and E. Potter (eds.) *Feminist Epistemologies*. New York 1993.

32   E. Said, *Orientalism*, London 1978.

33   R. D'Andrade, *Development of Cognitive Anthropology*, Cambridge 1995; Worsley, *Knowledges*; F. Barth, 'An anthropology of knowledge', *Current Anthropology* 43 (2002), 1–18; N. Adell, *Anthropologie des savoirs*, Paris 2011.

34   B. Latour and S. Woolgar, *Laboratory Life*, Beverly Hills CA, 1979; K. Knorr-Cetina, *The Manufacture of Knowledge*, Oxford 1981; B. Latour, *The Making of Law: An ethnography of the Conseil d'Etat*, Cambridge 2010. General reflections in Y. Elkanah, 'A programmatic attempt at an anthropology of knowledge', in E. Mendelsohn and Y. Elkanah (eds.) *Sciences and Cultures*, Dordrecht 1981.

35   C. Renfrew and E. Zubrow (eds.) *The Ancient Mind: Elements of Cognitive Archaeology*, Cambridge 1994; M. A. Abramiuk, *The Foundations of Cognitive Archaeology*. Cambridge MA 2012, 157–214.

36   J. W. Crampton and S. Elden (eds.) *Space, Knowledge and Power: Foucault and Geography*. Basingstoke 2007.

37 J. Golinski, *Making Natural Knowledge* (1998), 2nd edn Cambridge 2005, 79–102; D. N. Livingstone, *Putting Science in its Place: Geographies of Scientific Knowledge*, Chicago IL 2003.
38 I. Nonaka and H. Takeuchi, *The Knowledge-Creating Company*, New York 1995; K. J. Arrow, 'The economics of information', *Empirica* 23 (1996), 119–28, 125.
39 L. Bently and B. Sherman, *Intellectual Property*, Oxford 2004.
40 W. Mignolo, 'The geopolitics of knowledge and the colonial difference', *Social Epistemology* 19 (2005, 111–27; K. Dodds, *Geopolitics: A Very Short Introduction*, Oxford 2007, 115–72.
41 J. C. Scott, *Seeing Like a State*, New Haven CN 1999, especially 309–41.
42 W. D. Mignolo, *Local Histories/Global Designs: Coloniality, Subaltern Knowledges and Border Thinking*, Princeton NJ 2000; R. J. C. Young, *Postcolonialism: A Very Short Introduction*, Oxford, 2003; L. Tapia, *La producción del conocimiento local*, La Paz 2002 (*biblioteca.clacso.edu.ar/Bolivia/cides-umsa/20120906015335/tapia.pdf*).
43 R. N. Proctor and L. Schiebinger (eds.) *Agnotology: The Making and Unmaking of Ignorance*, Stanford, 2008; R. Wallis (ed.) *On the Margins of Science: The Social Construction of Rejected Knowledge*, Keele 1979; P. Burke, *A Social History of Knowledge* vol. 2 (Cambridge, 2012), 139–59.

2 Concepts

1 N. Stehr and R. Grundmann, *Knowledge: Critical Concepts*, 4 vols., London 2005, is a valuable anthology of concepts and criticisms.
2 T. F. Gieryn, 'Boundary-work and the demarcation of science from non-science: Strains and interests in professional ideologies of scientists', *American Sociological Review* 48 (1983), 781–95; R. Wallis (ed.) *On the Margins of Science: The Social Construction of Rejected Knowledge*. Keele 1979; P. Burke, *A Social History of Knowledge* vol. 2, 151–9.
3 P. Bourdieu, *Homo Academicus* (1984), English trans. Stanford 1988, especially 20–39.
4 Bourdieu, *Homo Academicus*, 40–8. On Italy, D. Moss, 'When patronage meets meritocracy', *Archives Européennes de Sociologie* 53 (2012), 205–30.
5 P. Burke, *The French Historical Revolution: The Annales School, 1929–2014*, 2nd edn Cambridge 2015, 36–72.
6 H. Innis, *Empire and Communications*, Oxford 1950.

7   H. Blumenberg, *The Legitimacy of the Modern Age* (1966), English trans. Cambridge MA 1983, 229–453, at 384; L. Daston, 'Curiosity in early modern science', *Word and Image* 11 (1995), 391–404, 391.

8   N. Kenny, *The Uses of Curiosity in Early Modern France and Germany*, Oxford 2004, 184.

9   N. Elias, 'Scientific establishments', in H. Martins, N. Elias and R. Whitley (eds.) *Scientific Establishments and Hierarchies*, Dordrecht 1982, 3–69; Bourdieu, *Homo Academicus*; T. Becher, *Academic Tribes and Territories: Intellectual Enquiry and the Cultures of Disciplines*, Milton Keynes 1989.

10   G. E. R. Lloyd, *Disciplines in the Making*, Oxford 2009, 172.

11   A. Blok, *The Innovators: The Blessings of Set-Backs*, Cambridge 2015.

12   P. B. Paulus and B. A. Nijstad (eds.) *Group Creativity: Innovation Through Collaboration*, Oxford 2003; S. Page, *The Difference*, Princeton NJ 2007.

13   C. Charle, *Naissance des 'intellectuels' 1880–1900*, Paris 1990.

14   R. Pipes (ed.) *The Russian Intelligentsia*, New York 1960.

15   T. Gelfand, 'The origins of a modern concept of medical specialization', *Bulletin of the History of Medicine* 50 (1976), 511–35.

16   P. Burke, 'The polymath: A cultural and social history of an intellectual species', in D. F. Smith and H. Philsooph (eds.) *Explorations in Cultural History: Essays for Peter McCaffery*, Aberdeen 2010, 67–79.

17   J. M. Ziman, *Knowing Everything about Nothing: Specialization and Change in Scientific Careers*, Cambridge 1987.

18   J. Soll, *The Information Master: Jean-Baptiste Colbert's Secret State Intelligence System*, Ann Arbor 2009, 7.

19   J. Gascoigne, *Science in the Service of Empire: Joseph Banks, the British State and the Uses of Science in the Age of Revolution*, Cambridge 1998.

20   B. vom Brocke, *Hochschul- und Wissenschaftspolitik in Preussen und im Deutsche Kaiserreich 1882–1907: Das 'System Althoff'*, Stuttgart 1980.

21   V. Berghahn, *America and the Intellectual Cold Wars in Europe*, Princeton NJ 2001.

22   F. Machlup, *The Production and Distribution of Knowledge in the United States*, Princeton NJ 1962; D. Bell, *The Coming of Post-Industrial Society*, London 1974.

23   P. F. Drucker, *Post-Capitalist Society*, Oxford 1993; I. Nonaka and H. Takeuchi, *The Knowledge Creating Company*, New

York 1995; T. A. Stewart, *Intellectual Capital: The New Wealth of Organizations*, London 1997.

24 M. Castells, *The Rise of the Network Society*, Oxford 1996.

25 J. L. van Zanden, *The Long Road to the Industrial Revolution*, Leiden 2009, 69–91.

26 R. Darnton, 'An early information society: News and the media in eighteenth-century Paris', *American Historical Review* 105 (2000), 1–35.

27 S. J. Pyne, *Voyager: Seeking Newer Worlds in the Third Great Age of Discovery*, New York 2010; M. D. Grmek, 'La troisième revolution scientifique', *Revue Médicale de la Suisse Romande* 119 (1999), 955–9; J. Greenwood, *The Third Industrial Revolution*, Rochester NY 1996.

28 M. Foucault, *Power/Knowledge: Selected Interviews and Other Writings, 1972–1977*, Brighton 1980, 114, 131; E. Said, *Orientalism*, London 1978, 195; E. Shils, 'The order of learning in the United States', in A. Oleson and J. Voss (eds.) *The Organization of Knowledge in Modern America, 1860–1920*, Baltimore 1979, 19–47; T. Varis, 'World information order', *Instant Research on Peace and Violence* 6 (1976), 143–7; C. Bayly, *Empire and Information: Intelligence Gathering and Social Communication in India, 1780–1870*, Cambridge 1996, 3, 7n; H. De Weerdt, 'Byways in the imperial Chinese information order', *Harvard Journal of Asiatic Studies* 66 (2006), 145–88.

29 F. Waquet, *Parler comme un livre*, Paris 2003.

30 Shils, 'Order of learning'.

31 A. Briggs and P. Burke, *A Social History of the Media* (2002), 3rd edn, Cambridge 2010.

32 H. F. Cohen, *How Modern Science Came into the World*, Amsterdam 2010; T. Huff, *Intellectual Curiosity and the Scientific Revolution: A Global Perspective*, Cambridge 2011.

33 G. E. R. Lloyd, *The Ambitions of Curiosity: Understanding the World in Ancient Greece and China*, Cambridge 2002.

34 H. Inalcık, *The Ottoman Empire: The Classical Age, 1300–1600*, London, 1973.

35 M. Foucault, *The Order of Things: An Archaeology of the Human Sciences* (1966), English trans. London 1970, preface.

36 R. D'Andrade, *The Development of Cognitive Anthropology*, Cambridge 1995; R. Bulmer, 'Why is the cassowary not a bird?' *Man* 2 (1967), 5–25.

37 H. Zedelmaier and M. Mulsow (eds.) *Die Praktiken der Gelehrsamkeit in der Frühen Neuzeit*, Tübingen 2001; D. Gardey, *Écrire, calculer, classer: comment une révolution de*

papier a transformé les sociétés contemporaines (1800–1940), Paris 2008, 25–70; A. Blair, *Too Much to Know: Managing Scholarly Information before the Modern Age*, New Haven CN 2010; P. Burke, 'The cultural history of intellectual practices: An overview', in J. Fernández Sebastián (ed.) *Political Concepts and Time*, Santander 2011, 103–27.

38 H. Perkin, *The Rise of Professional Society: England since 1880*, London 1989; A. Abbott, *The System of Professions*, Chicago IL 1988.

39 L. Veysey, *The Emergence of the American University*, Chicago IL 1965, 57–64; A. Abbott, *System of Professions*.

40 G. Stevenson and J. Kramer-Greene, *Melvil Dewey, the Man and the Classification*, Albany, NY 1983.

41 P. den Boer, *History as a Profession: The Study of History in France, 1818–1914* (1987), English trans. Princeton NJ 1998; D. R. Kelley, 'Johann Sleidan and the origins of history as a profession', *Journal of Modern History* 52 (1980), 577–98.

42 R. B. Townsend, *History's Babel: Scholarship, Professionalization and the Historical Enterprise in the United States, 1880–1940*, Chicago IL 2013.

43 R. M. McLeod (ed.) *Government and Expertise: Specialists, Administrators and Professionals, 1860–1919*, Cambridge 1988; R. Grundmann and N. Stehr, *The Power of Scientific Knowledge: From Research to Public Policy*. Cambridge 2012, 22–64.

44 R. Dilley and T. Kirsch (eds.) *Regimes of Ignorance*, Oxford 2015.

45 M. Twellmann, *Nichtwissen als Ressource*, Baden-Baden 2014.

46 W. Scott, 'Ignorance and revolution', in J. H. Pittock and A. Wear (eds.) *Interpretation and Cultural History*, London 1991, 235–68, 241; A. Tooze, *Statistics and the German State, 1900–1945: The Making of Modern Economic Knowledge*, Cambridge 2001, 84.

47 R. Dilley, 'The construction of ethnographic knowledge in a colonial context', in M. Harris (ed.) *Ways of Knowing*, Oxford 2007, 139–57, 147.

48 Foucault, *Power/Knowledge*, 63–77.

49 M. de Certeau, *The Writing of History* (1975), English trans. New York 1988.

50 M. Foucault, *The Birth of the Clinic: An Archaeology of Medical Perception* (1963), English trans. London 1973; W. Mignolo, 'The geopolitics of knowledge and the colonial difference', *Social Epistemology* 19 (2005), 111–27.

51 S. Van Damme, *Paris, capital philosophique de la Fronde à la revolution*, Paris 2005.

52 G. Basalla, 'The spread of Western science' (1967) rpr. W. K. Storey (ed.) *Scientific Aspects of European Expansion*, Aldershot 1996, 1–22; B. Latour, *Science in Action*, Cambridge MA 1987; H. Jöns, 'Centre of calculation', in J. Agnew and D. Livingstone (eds.), *The Sage Handbook of Geographical Knowledge*, Thousand Oaks CA 2011, 158–70.

53 K. Raj, *Relocating Modern Science. Circulation and the Construction of Knowledge in South Asia and Europe, 1650–1900*, Basingstoke 2007.

54 M. Bloch, *The Royal Touch* (1924), English trans. London 1973.

55 K. Mannheim, *Conservatism: A Contribution to the Sociology of Knowledge* (1927), English trans. London 1986.

56 L. Fleck, *Genesis and Development of a Scientific Fact* (1935), English trans. Chicago IL 1979, 39, 141. Cf. R. S. Cohen and T. Schnelle, *Cognition and Fact: Materials on Ludwik Fleck*, Dordrecht 1986.

57 J. R. Short, *Cartographic Encounters: Indigenous Peoples and the Exploration of the New World*, London 2009, offers a range of examples.

58 E. Said, *Orientalism*, London 1978, 2–3, 6–7, 43.

59 C. G. Gillispie, 'Scientific aspects of the French Egyptian expedition', *Proceedings of the American Philosophical Society* 133 (1989), 447–74; A. Godlewska, 'The Napoleonic survey of Egypt: A masterpiece of cartographic compilation and early nineteenth-century fieldwork', *Cartographica* 25 (1988), 1–171.

60 J. M. Mackenzie, 'Edward Said and the historians', *Nineteenth-Century Contexts* 18 (1994), 9–25; R. Irwin, *For Lust of Knowing: The Orientalists and their Enemies*, London 2006, 2–4, 277–9.

61 Said, *Orientalism*, 164; L. Ahmed, *Edward W. Lane*, London 1978, 111. Cf. Irwin, *For Lust of Knowing*, 163–6.

62 B. S. Cohn, *Colonialism and its Forms of Knowledge*, Princeton NJ 1996, 5–11, 53–6; C. Bayly, *Empire and Information: Intelligence Gathering and Social Communication in India, 1780–1870*, Cambridge 1996, 8, 49–50.

63 M. S. Dodson, *Orientalism, Empire and National Culture*, Basingstoke 2007, emphasizes the role of the Indian *pandits*.

64 T. R. Trautmann, 'Inventing the history of South India', in D. Ali (ed.) *Invoking the Past: The Uses of History in South Asia*, Delhi 1999, 36–54, 36; E. F. Irschick, *Dialogue and History: Constructing South India, 1795–1895*, Berkeley 1994, 8.

65 M. Polanyi, *Personal Knowledge*, Chicago IL 1958; *The Tacit Dimension*, Chicago IL 1966. Cf. M. T. Mitchell, *Michael Polanyi: The Art of Knowing*, Wilmington, DE 2006.

66 P. Bourdieu, *Outline; Science of Science.*

67 P. Bourdieu and R. Chartier, *Le sociologue.*

68 L. Roberts and I. Inkster (eds.) 'The mindful hand', *History of Technology* 29 (2009), 103–211; L. Roberts, S. Schaffer and P. Dear (eds.) *The Mindful Hand: Inquiry and Invention from the Late Renaissance to Early Industrialization*, Amsterdam 2007; P. Smith, *The Body of the Artisan: Art and Experience in the Scientific Revolution*, Chicago IL 2004, 142. Cf. R. Sennett, *The Craftsman*, London 2008; D. Raven, 'Artisanal knowledge', *Acta Baltica Historiae et Philosophiae Scientiarum* 1 (2013), 5–34.

69 T. Marchand, *Minaret Building and Apprenticeship in Yemen*, Richmond 2001.

70 T. Marchand, 'Embodied cognition and communication: Studies with British fine woodworkers', *Journal of the Royal Anthropological Institute* (2010), 100–20.

71 http://news.columbia.edu/pamelasmith.

72 E. Zilsel, *Social Origins of Modern Science*, eds. D. Raven, W. Krohn and R. S. Cohen, Dordrecht 2003 (essays first published in the early 1940s; P. Rossi, *Philosophy, Technology and the Arts in the Early Modern Era* (1962), English trans. New York 1970; P. O. Long, *Artisan/Practitioners and the Rise of the New Sciences, 1400–1600.* Corvallis OR 2011.

73 P. Becker and W. Clark (eds.) *Little Tools of Knowledge: Historical Essays on Academic and Bureaucratic Practices*, Ann Arbor 2001.

74 M. S. Phillips and G. Schochet (eds.) *Questions of Tradition*, Toronto 2004, an invaluable introduction.

75 E. J. Hobsbawm and T. Ranger (eds.) *The Invention of Tradition*, Cambridge 1983.

76 A. Warburg, *The Renewal of Pagan Antiquity* (1932) English trans. Los Angeles 1999.

77 Burke, *The French Historical Revolution.*

78 J. Harwood, 'National styles in science', *Isis* 78 (1987), 390–414.

79 F. Barth et al., *One Discipline, Four Ways: British, German, French and American Anthropology*, Chicago IL 2005; cf. S. Z. Klausner and V. M. Lidz (eds.) *The Nationalization of Social Science*, Philadelphia 1986.

80 Umberto Eco, *Mouse or Rat? Translation as Negotiation*, London 2003.

81 Cohen, *How Modern Science Came into the World*.
82 D. Schön, *Displacement of Concepts*, London 1963.
83 D. Fleming and B. Bailyn (eds.) *The Intellectual Migration: Europe and America, 1930–1960*, Cambridge MA 1969; L. A. Coser, *Refugee Scholars in America: Their Impact and their Experiences*, New Haven CN 1984.
84 R. Lindner, *The Reportage of Urban Culture: Robert Park and the Chicago School* (1990), English trans. Cambridge 1996.

3 Processes

1 L. Daston, 'Historical epistemology', in J. Chandler, A. I. Davidson and H. Harootunian (eds.) *Questions of Evidence*, Chicago IL 1994, 282–7.
2 L. Daston and P. Galison, *Objectivity*, New York 2007, 17, 51.
3 P. Novick, *That Noble Dream: The 'Objectivity Question' and the American Historical Profession*, Cambridge 1988, 252–64.
4 Quoted in A. Pettegree, *The Invention of News*, New Haven CN 2014, 267.
5 M. Schudson, *Sociology of News*, New York 2003, 83.
6 N. Elias, *Involvement and Detachment*, Oxford 1987; M. S. Phillips, *On Historical Distance*, New Haven CN 2013.
7 R. L. Euben, *Journeys to the Other Shore: Muslim and Western Travelers in Search of Knowledge*. Princeton NJ 2006.
8 L. Daston and E. Lunbeck, *Histories of Scientific Observation*, Chicago IL 2011, i; R. Hoozee (ed.) *British Vision: Observation and Imagination in British Art, 1750–1950*, Ghent 2007, 12.
9 O. MacDonagh, 'The nineteenth-century revolution in Government: A reappraisal', *Historical Journal* 1 (1958), 52–67; cf. R. M. MacLeod, *Government and Expertise: Specialists, Administrators and Professionals, 1860–1919*, Cambridge 1988.
10 C. Ginzburg, *Clues, Myths, and the Historical Method* (1978), English trans. Baltimore 1989.
11 J. Platt, *A History of Sociological Research Methods in America, 1920–1960*, Cambridge 1996.
12 J. Delbourgo and N. Dew, *Science and Empire in the Atlantic World*, London 2008; D. Bleichmar, *Visible Empire: Botanical Expeditions and Visual Culture in the Hispanic Enlightenment*, Chicago IL 2012.

13   B. Smith, *European Vision and the South Pacific*, Oxford 1960, 16.

14   Smith, *European Vision*, 48; N. Thomas, *Discoveries: The Voyages of Captain Cook*, London 2003, 63.

15   Ibid., 53, 71, 79, 82, 105, 125, 129, 149.

16   Ibid., 108.

17   R. Head, 'Knowing like a state: The transformation of political knowledge in Swiss archives 1450–1770', *Journal of Modern History* 75 (2003), 745–82; F. De Vivo, 'Ordering the archive in early modern Venice', *Archival Science* 10 (2010), 231–48; A. Blair and J. Milligan, (eds.) 'Toward a cultural history of archives', special issue of *Archival Science* 7 (2007).

18   A good introduction to the history of libraries is M. Battles, *Library: An Unquiet History*, Cambridge MA 2003.

19   J. Raven (ed.) *Lost Libraries*, London 2004; Burke, *A Social History of Knowledge* vol. 2, 139–59.

20   F. Yates, *The Art of Memory*, London 1966.

21   H. G. Schulte-Albert, 'Gottfried Wilhelm Leibniz and Library Classification', *Journal of Library History* 6 (1971), 133–52.

22   A. Wright, *Cataloging the World: Paul Otlet and the Birth of the Information Age*, New York 2014.

23   A. Halavais, *Search Engine Society*, Cambridge 2009.

24   B. W. Ogilvie, *The Science of Describing*, Chicago IL 2007.

25   S. Alpers, *Art of Describing*, Chicago IL 1983.

26   Hoozee, *British Vision*, 12.

27   J.-C. Perrot and S. Woolf, *State and Statistics in France, 1789–1815*, New York 1984.

28   T. Frängsmyr, J. H. Heilbron and R. H. Rider (eds.) *The Quantifying Spirit in the Eighteenth Century*, London 1990; E. R. Tufte, *The Visual Display of Quantitative Information*, Cheshire CT 1983.

29   I. Jacknis, 'Franz Boas and exhibits', in *Objects and Others*, ed. George W. Stocking, Madison WI 1985, 75–111.

30   G. Dumézil, *Mitra-Varuna* (1940), English trans. New York 1988.

31   P. Burke, 'Context in context', *Common Knowledge* 8: 1 (2002) 152–77.

32   E. Panofsky, 'Iconography and Iconology' (1932), English trans. in his *Meaning in the Visual Arts*, Garden City NY 1955.

33   L. Kramer, *Music as Cultural Practice, 1800–1900*, Berkeley CA 1990.

34 I. Hodder, *Reading the Past: Current Approaches to Interpretation in Archaeology*, Cambridge 1986; H. Johnsen and B. Olsen, 'Hermeneutics and archaeology', *American Antiquity* 57 (1992), 419–36.

35 C. Geertz, *The Interpretation of Cultures*, New York 1973.

36 E. Cassirer, *Das Erkenntnisproblem in der Philosophie und Wissenschaft der neueren Zeit*, Berlin 1911; L. Daston, 'Historical epistemology'; H. J. Rheinberger, *On Historicizing Epistemology* (2007) English trans. Stanford CA 2010; J. Chandler, A. I. Davidson and H. Harootunian (eds.) *Questions of Evidence: Proof, Practice and Persuasion Across the Disciplines*, Chicago IL 1994.

37 S. Shapin, A *Social History of Truth: Civility and Science in Seventeenth-Century England*, Chicago IL 1994.

38 E. Zilsel, *The Social Origins of Modern Science*, ed. D. Raven, W. Krohn and R. S. Cohen, Dordrecht 2000.

39 B. J. Shapiro, *A Culture of Fact: England 1550–1720*, Ithaca NY 2000, 8–33.

40 M. Clanchy, *From Memory to Written Record*, London 1979.

41 A. Fox and D. Woolf (eds.) *The Spoken Word: Oral Culture in Britain, 1500–1850*, Manchester 2003.

42 I. Hacking, *The Emergence of Probability*, Cambridge 1975; B. J. Shapiro, *'Beyond Reasonable Doubt': Historical Perspectives on the Anglo-American Law of Evidence*, Berkeley CA 1991.

43 E. J. Kenney, *Classical Text: Aspects of Editing in the Age of the Printed Book*, Berkeley CA 1974.

44 T. Khalidi, *Arabic Historical Thought in the Classical Period*, Cambridge 1994.

45 Shapiro, *Culture of Fact*, 107–9, 113.

46 M. Poovey, *A History of the Modern Fact: Problems of Knowledge in the Sciences of Wealth and Society*, Chicago IL 1998.

47 R. H. Popkin, *The History of Scepticism from Savonarola to Bayle* (1960), 3rd edn, Oxford 2003, 270; P. Burke, 'History, myth and fiction: Doubts and debates', *Oxford History of Historical Writing* vol. 3, ed. J. Rabasa et al., Oxford 2012, 261–81; B. Dooley, *The Social History of Skepticism*, Baltimore 1999, 9–44.

48 A. Grafton, *The Footnote*, London 1997, and C. Zerby, *The Devil's Details*, Montpellier VT 2002.

49 L. Mink, 'Narrative form as a cognitive instrument', in R. H. Canary and H. Kozicki (eds.) *The Writing of History*, Madison WI 1978, 129–49.

50   G. Beer, *Darwin's Plots: Evolutionary Narrative in Darwin, George Eliot and Nineteenth-Century Fiction*, London 1983.
51   P. Ricoeur, *Temps et Récit* vol. 1, Paris 1983, 208–17, at 208.
52   L. Stone, 'The revival of narrative', *Past and Present* 85 (1979), 3–24.
53   C. Geertz, *The Interpretation of Cultures*, 412–53.
54   K. G. Heider, 'The Rashomon effect', *American Anthropologist* 90 (1988), 73–81.
55   J. A. Secord, 'Knowledge in transit', *Isis* 95 (2004) 654–72; M. Elshakry, 'Knowledge in motion', *Isis* 99 (2008), 701–30.
56   A. Blair, *Too Much to Know: Managing Scholarly Information Before the Modern Age*, New Haven CN 2010.
57   C. M. Cipolla, 'The diffusion of innovations in early modern Europe', *Comparative Studies in Society and History* 14 (1972), 46–52; J. M. Ziman, 'Ideas move around inside people' (1974), rpr. his *Puzzles, Problems and Enigmas*, Cambridge 1981, 259–72.
58   L. Stone (ed.) *Schooling and Society*, Baltimore 1976; W. Rüegg, *History of the University in Europe*, 4 vols., Cambridge 1992–2011.
59   J. Berkey, *The Transmission of Knowledge in Medieval Cairo*, Princeton NJ 1992; M. Chamberlain, *Knowledge and Social Practice in Medieval Damascus*, Cambridge 1994.
60   F. Waquet, *Les enfants de Socrate: filiation intellectuelle et transmission du savoir, XVII–XXIe siècle*, Paris 2008.
61   F. Waquet, *Parler comme un livre: l'oralité et le savoir (XVIe–XXe siècle)*, Paris 2003.
62   P. Burke, 'From the disputation to power point: Staging academic knowledge in Europe, 1100–2000', in H. Blume et al. (eds.) *Inszenierung und Gedächtnis*, Bielefeld 2014, 119–31.
63   J. W. Chaffee, *The Thorny Gates of Learning in Sung China: A Social History of Examinations*, Cambridge 1985; B. A. Elman, *A Cultural History of Civil Examinations in Late Imperial China*, Berkeley CA 2000.
64   R. M. MacLeod (ed.) *Days of Judgement: Science, Examinations and the Organization of Knowledge in Late Victorian England*, Driffield 1982; C. Stray, 'From oral to written examinations: Cambridge, Oxford and Dublin 1700–1914', *History of Universities* 20 (2005), 76–129.
65   J. Clifford, *Person and Myth: Maurice Leenhardt in the Melanesian World*, Berkeley CA 1982.
66   Euben, *Journeys*, 90–133.

67 P. Chakrabarti, *Western Science in Modern India*, Delhi 2004; G. Prakash, *Another Reason: Science and the Imagination of Modern India*, Princeton NJ 1999; Dodson, *Orientalism*.

68 M. J. Franklin, *Orientalist Jones*, Oxford 2011, 36–42; T. R. Trautmann, 'Hullabaloo about Telugu', *South Asia Research* 19, 53–70.

69 H. Fischer-Tiné, *Pidgin-Knowledge*, Zurich 2013; Prakash, *Another Reason*, 54–5.

70 Trautmann, 'Hullabaloo', 67.

71 L. A. Coser, *Refugee Scholars in America: Their Impact and their Experiences*, New Haven CN 1984; D. Fleming and B. Bailyn (eds.) *The Intellectual Migration: Europe and America, 1930–1960*, Cambridge MA 1969.

72 Burke, *Social History of Knowledge*, 208–11.

73 S. J. Harris, 'Confession-building, long-distance networks, and the organisation of Jesuit science', *Early Modern European Science* 1 (1996), 287–318; M. Ultee, 'The Republic of Letters: Learned correspondence 1680–1720', *The Seventeenth Century* 2 (1987), 95–112.

74 P. Burke, 'The Republic of Letters as a communication system', *Media History* (2012), 1–13.

75 G. Basalla, 'The spread of Western science' (1967), rpr. W. K. Storey (ed.) *Scientific Aspects of European Expansion*, Aldershot 1996, 1–22.

76 S. Sivasundaram, 'Sciences and the global', *Isis* 101 (2010), 146–58, at 154. Cf. M. Harrison, 'Networks of knowledge', in D. Peers and N. Gooptu (eds.) *India and the British Empire*, Oxford 2012, 191–211.

77 K. Raj, *Relocating Modern Science. Circulation and the Construction of Knowledge in South Asia and Europe, 1650–1900*, Basingstoke 2007.

78 Fischer-Tiné, *Pidgin-Knowledge*, 57–61.

79 Ibid., 18–33.

80 D. Keene, *The Japanese Discovery of Europe 1720–1830* (1952), revd edn Stanford CA 1969; Fujita quoted in C. Hill, *National History and the World of Nations*, Durham NC 2008, 66.

81 P. Burke, 'Translating knowledge, translating cultures', in M. North (ed.) *Kultureller Austausch: Bilanz und Perspektiven der Frühneuzeitforschung*, Cologne 2009, 69–77.

82 M. Bravo, *Accuracy of Ethnoscience*, Manchester 1996, 2.

83 A. W. Daum, *Wissenschaftspopularisierung in 19 Jahrhundert*, Munich 1998; B. Lightman, *Victorian Popularizers of Science: Designing Nature for New Audiences*, Chicago IL 2007.

84 J. A. Secord, *Victorian Sensation: The Extraordinary Publication, Reception, and Secret Authorship of Vestiges of the Natural History of Creation*, Chicago IL 2000.

85 P. Burke and J. McDermott (eds.) *The Book Worlds of East Asia and Europe, 1450–1850: Connections and Comparisons*, Hong Kong, forthcoming.

86 M. E. Berry, *Japan in Print: Information and Nation in the Early Modern Period*, Berkeley CA 2006.

87 P. Kornicki, *The Book in Japan: A Cultural History from the Beginnings to the 19th Century*, Leiden 1998, 320–62; T. Brook, 'Censorship in 18th-century China: A view from the book trade', *Canadian Journal of History* 23 (1988), 177–96.

88 P. Grendler, 'Printing and censorship', in C. Schmitt and Q. Skinner (eds.) *The Cambridge History of Renaissance Philosophy*, Cambridge 1988, 25–53; M. Infelise, *I libri prohibiti da Gutenberg a l'Encyclopédie*, Rome and Bari 1999.

89 Dodson, *Orientalism*, 53.

90 D. Kahn, *The Codebreakers*, London 1978.

91 F. De Vivo, *Information and Communication in Venice: Rethinking Early Modern Politics*, Oxford 2007, 57–8.

92 J. Proust, *Diderot et l'Encyclopédie*, Paris 1962.

93 J. Gibbs, *Gorbachev's Glasnost*, College Station TX 1994.

94 Arrow, 'Economics of information', 125.

95 P. Burke, 'The bishop's questions and the people's religion', in *Historical Anthropology of Early Modern Europe*, Cambridge 1987, 40–7.

96 M. Friedrich, *Der lange Arm Roms? Globale Verwaltung und Kommunikation im Jesuitenorden 1540–1773*, Frankfurt 2011; 'Communication and bureaucracy in the early modern society of Jesus', *Zeitschrift für Schweizerische Religions und Kirchegeschichte* 101 (2007), 49–75.

97 E. Johansson, 'Literacy studies in Sweden', in Johansson (ed.) *Literacy and Society in a Historical Perspective*, Umeå 1973, 41–65.

98 D. E. Smith, *Texts, Facts and Femininity: Exploring the Relations of Ruling*, London 1990.

99 A. Brendecke, *Imperium und Empirie, Funktionen des Wissens in der spanischen Kolonialherrschaft*, Cologne 2009, 252ff and passim.

100 J. Soll, *The Information Master: Jean-Baptiste Colbert's Secret State Intelligence System*, Ann Arbor 2009, 72–3, 100, 104–12.

101 M. Moir, '*Kaghazi Raj*: Notes on the documentary basis of company rule, 1783–1858', *Indo-British Review* 21 (1983),

185–9; P. A. Kuhn, *Soulstealers: The Chinese Sorcery Scare of 1768*, Cambridge, MA 1990.

102 J. Caplan and J. Torpey (eds.) *Documenting Individual Identity*, Princeton NJ 2001; J. Torpey, *The Invention of the Passport*, Cambridge 2000.

103 E. Higgs, *The Information State in England: The Central Collection of Information on Citizens*, Basingstoke 2004, reviewed by V. Gatrell, *Journal of Historical Sociology* 18 (2005), 126–32.

104 J. Hoock and P. Jeannin, *Ars mercatoria*, 6 vols., Paderborn 1991.

105 L. Blussé and I. Ooms (eds.), *Kennis en Compagnie: de Vereenigde Oost-Indische Compagnie en de modern wetenschap*, Amsterdam 2002.

106 J. Yates, 'Business use of information and technology during the industrial age', in A. D. Chandler and J. W. Cortada (eds.) *A Nation Transformed by Information*, New York 2000, 107–36.

107 J. C. Scott, *Seeing like a State*, New Haven CN 1999; cf. B. Flyvbjerg, 'Phronesis and megaprojects', in B. Flyvbjerg, T. Landman and S. Schram (eds.) *Real Social Science: Applied Phronesis*, Cambridge 2012, 95–121.

4 Problems and Prospects

1 T. S. Kuhn, *The Structure of Scientific Revolutions*, Chicago IL 1962.

2 G. Bachelard (1934), *The Formation of the Scientific Mind*, English trans. Manchester 2002; G. Canguilhem, *Knowledge of Life* (1965), English trans. New York 2008.

3 M. Foucault, *The Archaeology of Knowledge* (1969), English trans. New York 1972.

4 S. Shapin, *The Scientific Revolution*, Chicago IL 1996.

5 G. G. Iggers, 'The crisis of the Rankean paradigm', in *Syracuse Scholar* 9 (1988), 43–50.

6 J. C. Heesterman, *The Inner Conflict of Tradition*, Chicago IL 1985; cf. M. S. Phillips and G. Schochet, *Questions of Tradition*, Toronto 2004.

7 L. Venuti, *The Translator's Invisibility*, New York 1995.

8 C. Charle, *Naissance des 'intellectuels'*, Paris 1990.

9 J. Le Goff, *Les intellectuels au Moyen Âge*, Paris 1957; J. Verger, *Les gens de savoir dans l' Europe de la fin du Moyen Âge*, Paris 1997, 2–3; P. Wormald and J. L. Nelson (eds.) *Lay*

Intellectuals in the Carolingian World, Cambridge 2007, 222, 248.

10 T. S. Kuhn, 'Remarks on incommensurability and translation', in R. R. Favretti, G. Sandri and R. Scazzieri (eds.) *Incommensurability and Translation*, Cheltenham 1999, 33–8.

11 K. Mannheim, *Ideology and Utopia* (1929), English trans. London 1936, 254; cf. R. K. Merton, 'Karl Mannheim' (1941), in *Social Theory and Social Structure*, 2nd edn, Glencoe 1957, 489–508.

12 Kuhn, *Structure of Scientific Revolutions*, 4; D. Bloor, *Knowledge and Social Imagery*, London 1976.

13 F. Barth, 'An anthropology of knowledge', *Current Anthropology* 43 (2002), 1–18, at 3.

14 B. Latour and S. Woolgar, *Laboratory Life*, Beverly Hills CA 1979.

15 L. Nader (ed.) *Naked Science: Anthropological Inquiries into Boundaries, Power and Knowledge*, New York 1996. Cf. M. Bravo, *The Accuracy of Ethnoscience*, Manchester 1996; L. M. Semali and J. L. Kincheloe (eds.) *What is Indigenous Knowledge?* New York 1999.

16 D. Christian, *Maps of Time: An Introduction to Big History*, Berkeley CA 2011, 182–4.

17 G. Beaujouan, 'The dark ages and the remnants of classical science', in R. Taton (ed.), *Ancient and Medieval Science* (1957), English trans. London 1963, 469–73.

18 R. W. Southern, *The Making of the Middle Ages*, London 1953, 210.

19 A. Blair, *Too Much to Know*, New Haven CN 2010.

20 Further details in P. Burke, *A Social History of Knowledge* vol. 2, Cambridge 2012, 139–83.

21 R. Rorty, *Philosophy and the Mirror of Nature*, Oxford 1980, 163. Cf N. Goodman, *Ways of Worldmaking*, Chicago IL 1978.

22 R. Chartier, *On the Edge of the Cliff*, Baltimore MD 1997.

23 J. Golinski, *Making Natural Knowledge* (1998), 2nd edn Cambridge 2005, ix and passim; D. N. Livingstone, *Putting Science in its Place: Geographies of Scientific Knowledge*, Chicago IL 2003.

24 P. Bourdieu, *Science of Science and Reflexivity* (2001), English trans. Cambridge 2004.

25 E. J. Hobsbawm and T. Ranger (eds.) *The Invention of Tradition*, Cambridge 1983.

26 N. Dirks, *Castes of Mind: Colonialism and the Making of Modern India*, Princeton NJ 2001, 5.

27 F. Barth, 'An anthropology of knowledge', *Current Anthropology* 43 (2002), 1–18, at 3; P. Bourdieu, *Homo Academicus* (1984), English trans. Stanford 1988.

28 K. Park, *Secrets of Women: Gender, Generation and the Origins of Human Dissection*, New York 2010.

29 L. Schiebinger, 'Nature's unruly body', in J. Bender and M. Marrinan (eds.) *Regimes of Description*, Stanford 2005, 25–43, at 35.

30 D. Haraway, 'Situated knowledges', *Feminist Studies* 14 (1988), 575–9.

31 A. B. Shteir, *Cultivating Women, Cultivating Science*, Baltimore MD, 1996.

32 B. G. Smith, *The Gender of History: Men, Women and Historical Practice*. Cambridge MA 1998, 1.

33 Smith, *Gender of History*, 207.

34 D. Landes, *The Wealth and Poverty of Nations*, New York 1998, xix, 200, 470, 472. Cf. P. O'Brien, 'Historical foundations for a global perspective on the emergence of a West European regime for the discovery, development and diffusion of useful and reliable knowledge', *Journal of Global History* 8 (2013), 1–24.

35 P. Paret, *The Cognitive Challenge of War: Prussia 1806*, Princeton NJ 2009.

36 K. Park and A. Ragab, *Knowledge on the Move*, a course taught at Harvard. The same title was given to a summer school in Heidelberg in 2010, organized by J. Kurtz and M. Hofmann.

37 S. Sivasundaram, 'Sciences and the global', *Isis* 101 (2010), 146–58; D. Woolf, *A Global History of History*, Cambridge 2011.

38 L. Wacquant, *Body and Soul: Notebooks of an Apprentice Boxer*, New York 2004; G. Downey, *Learning Capoeira: Lessons in Cunning from an Afro-Brazilian Art*, Oxford 2005.

39 Christian, *Maps of Time*, 182.

40 Ibid., 207, 306.

41 V. G. Childe, *Social Worlds of Knowledge*, London 1949.

42 T. Marchand, 'Embodied cognition: Studies with British fine woodworkers', *Journal of the Royal Anthropological Institute* (2010), 100–20; C. Renfrew and E. Zubrow (eds.) *The Ancient Mind: Elements of Cognitive Archaeology*. Cambridge 1994.

43 E. B. Tribble and N. Keene, *Cognitive Ecologies and the History of Remembering*, Basingstoke 2011.

44 Christian, *Maps of Time*; D. L. Smail, *On Deep History and the Brain*, Berkeley CA 2008; cf. G. E. R. Lloyd, *Cognitive Variations: Reflections on the Unity and Diversity of the Human Mind*, Oxford 2004.

45 U. Neisser and R. Fivush (eds.) *The Remembering Self: Construction and Accuracy in the Self-Narrative*, Cambridge 1994, 6.

46 A. Portelli, *The Death of Luigi Trastulli and Other Stories: Form and Meaning in Oral History*, Albany NY 1991; A. Thomson, *Anzac Memories: Living with the Legend*, Melbourne 1994.

Timeline: Studies of Knowledge, a Select Chronology

1605 Francis Bacon, *Advancement of Learning*

1718 Stolle, *Anleitung zur Histoire der Gelahrtheit* (Introduction to the history of learning)

1781 Meiners, *Geschichte des Ursprungs, Fortgangs und Verfalls der Wissenschaften in Griechenland und Rom* (History of the origin, progress and decline of the sciences in Greece and Rome)

1795 Condorcet, *Esquisse d'un tableau historique des progrès de l'esprit humain* (Sketch for an historical picture of the progress of the human mind)

1832 Comte asked Guizot to found a chair in history of science

1873 Candolle, *Histoire des sciences et des savants* (History of the sciences and scientists)

1892 Chair in the history of science, Collège de France

1923 History of Science Society, USA

1925 Mannheim, 'Das Problem einer Soziologie des Wissens' (The problem of a sociology of knowledge)

1926 Scheler, *Die Wissensformen und die Gesellschaft* (Forms of knowledge in society)

1935 Fleck, *Entstehung und Entwicklung einer Wissenschaftlichen Tatsache* (Genesis and development of a scientific fact)

1938   Merton, *Science, Technology and Society in Seventeenth Century England*
1957   Le Goff, *Les intellectuels au moyen age* (The intellectuals in the Middle Ages)
1960   Popkin, *History of Scepticism*
1962   Machlup, *The Production and Distribution of Knowledge in the United States*
1966   Foucault, *Les mots et les choses* (The order of things)
1969   Foucault, *L'archéologie du savoir* (The archaeology of knowledge)
1974   Detienne and Vernant, *Les ruses de l'intelligence* (Cunning intelligence in Greek culture and society)
1976   Foucault, *La volonté de savoir* (The will to knowledge)
1978   Edward Said, *Orientalism*
1979   Bruno Latour/Steve Woolgar, *Laboratory Life*
1979   Oleson and Voss, *The Organization of Knowledge in Modern America*
1983   Shapiro, *Probability and Certainty in Seventeenth-Century England*
1985   Shapin and Schaffer, *Leviathan and the Air-Pump*
1988   MacLeod, *Government and Expertise*
1988   Haraway, 'Situated knowledges'
1989   Schiebinger, *The Mind has no Sex?*
1989   Brown, *Knowledge is Power*
1992   Ringer, *Fields of Knowledge*
1994   Shapin, *A Social History of Truth*
1996   Bayly, *Empire and Information*
1996   Cohn, *Colonialism and its Forms of Knowledge*
1997   Worsley, *Knowledges: What Different Peoples Make of the World*
1998   Golinski, *Making Natural Knowledge*
1998   Poovey, *A History of the Modern Fact*
1999   Dooley, *The Social History of Skepticism*
2000   Burke, *A Social History of Knowledge from Gutenberg to Diderot*
2000   Mignolo, *Local Histories/Global Designs*
2000   Lander, *La colonialidad del saber* (The coloniality of knowledge)
2000   Chandler and Cortada, *A Nation Transformed by Information*
2000   Pickstone, *Ways of Knowing*

2000   Shapiro, *A Culture of Fact*
2001   Zedelmaier and Mulsow, *Die Praktiken der Gelehrs-amkeit in der Frühen Neuzeit* (Learned practices in early modern Europe)
2001   Headrick, *When Information Came of Age*
2002   Lloyd, *The Ambitions of Curiosity*
2004   Van Dülmen and Rauschenbach, *Macht des Wissens* (The power of Knowledge)
2004   Higgs, *The Information State in England*
2004   Kenny, *The Uses of Curiosity*
2005   Daunton, *The Organization of Knowledge in Victorian Britain*
2005   Van Damme, *Paris, capital philosophique* (Paris, the capital of philosophy)
2006   Berry, *Japan in Print*
2007   De Vivo, *Information and Communication in Venice*
2007   Jacob, *Lieux de Savoir* (Realms of Knowledge)
2007   König and Whitmarsh, *Ordering Knowledge in the Roman Empire*
2008   Gardey, *Écrire, calculer, classer* (Writing, calculating, classifying)
2008   Romano, *Rome et la science moderne* (Rome and modern science)
2009   Brendecke, *Imperium und Empirie* (Empire and empiricism)
2009   Lloyd, *Disciplines in the Making*
2009   Soll, *The Information Master*
2010   Blair, *Too Much to Know*
2010   Bod, *De Vergeten Wetenschappen* (The forgotten sciences)
2010   Daston and Galison, *Objectivity*
2011   Daston and Lunbeck, *Histories of Scientific Observation*
2011   Huff, *Intellectual Curiosity and the Scientific Revolution*
2011   Friedrich, *Der Lang Arme Roms?* (The long arm of Rome)
2012   Burke, *A Social History of Knowledge: From the Encyclopaedia to Wikipedia*
2012   Mulsow, *Präkares Wissen* (Precarious knowledge)
2013   Fischer-Tiné, *Pidgin-Knowledge*
2014   Turner, *Philology*

Further Reading

I. F. McNeely and L. Wolverton, *Reinventing Knowledge: From Alexandria to the Internet* (New York, 2008) offers a short and lively introduction to the history of knowledge over the last two thousand years. For the last five hundred, P. Burke, *A Social History of Knowledge from Gutenberg to Diderot* (Cambridge, 2000); *A Social History of Knowledge from the Encyclopédie to Wikipedia* (Cambridge, 2012).

Some studies of knowledge made in other disciplines are essential for historians. J. Nagel, *Knowledge* (Oxford, 2014) offers a short and lucid introduction to problems of epistemology. K. Mannheim's *Essays on the Sociology of Knowledge* (English trans. London 1952) are fundamental, especially chapter 4, 'The problem of a sociology of knowledge'. In the case of Foucault, it might be best to read a collection of interviews with him: *Power/Knowledge* (Brighton, 1980) before turning to his 'Archaeology of knowledge' in the *Order of Things* (English trans. London 1970). D. Haraway's 'Situated knowledge' first appeared in *Feminist Studies* 14 (1988), 575–99. B. Latour's discussion of 'centres of calculation' can be found in his *Science in Action* (Milton Keynes, 1987). P. Bourdieu's final reflections on knowledge can be found in his *Science of Science and Reflexivity* (English trans. Cambridge 2004). For a lucid exposition of a geographical approach, see D. Livingstone, *Putting Science in its Place*

(Chicago, 2003). For an anthropological point of view, see F. Barth, 'An anthropology of knowledge', *Current Anthropology* 43 (2002), 1–11.

The endnotes to this book offer suggestions for further reading on many topics.

Index

Abelard, Peter, 79
Acton, Lord, 45–6
agency, 118–19
Ahmed, Leila, 36
Akutagawa, Ryonosuke, 76
al-Beruni, 68
al-Kindi, 93
al-Tatawi, Rifa'a, 83
Althoff, Frederick, 24
Ambrose, 17
anachronism, 111–12
analysis, 57–8, 75
Annales School, 41, 75, 124
anthropology, 11–13, 29, 32,
    38, 41, 60, 62, 65–6, 74,
    76–7, 82, 105, 113, 123–4
archaeology, 12, 65, 124
archives, 52–4, 104, 110
area studies, 23, 62
Aristotle, 17, 89, 122
Arrow, Kenneth, 97
artisans (see also
    knowhow), 38–9, 42, 55,
    61–2, 86, 93, 95
Astruc, Jean, 72
Aubrey, John, 40, 58
Augustine, 17

authorities, 15
autopsy, 67

Bachelard, Gaston, 109, 116
Bacon, Francis, 3, 10, 18, 24,
    33, 62, 67, 69
Bakhtin, Mikhail, 119
Banks, Joseph, 18, 24, 51
baroni, 16
Barth, Fredrik, 12, 113, 118
Basalla, George, 87
Bayly, Christopher, 37
Beard, Charles, 45, 121
Beard, Mary, 121
Becker, Carl, 45
Bede, 115
Bell, Daniel, 25
Berkey, Jonathan, 78–9
Berry, MaryElizabeth, 91
Bertillon, Alphonse, 60
bias, 71
Bible, 65, 69, 100
Bierling, Friedrich, 71
Bloch, Marc, 34–5, 41
Blok, Anton, 20
Bloor, David, 113
Boas, Franz, 62

Bodin, Jean, 122
Bopp, Franz, 63
Borges, Jorge Luis, 29
botany (see also Linnaeus),
    58–9, 121
Bourdieu, Pierre, 10–11, 16,
    35, 38, 117–18
Brand, Stewart, 97
Braudel, Fernand, 16, 41, 75,
    82–3
Brendecke, Arndt, 100
Buckland, William, 80
Burckhardt, Jacob, 66
bureaucratization, 30, 49, 59,
    100–1, 103
Butterfield, Herbert, 69

Canguilhem, Georges, 109
Carlyle, Thomas, 46
Cartright, Julia, 121
Casaubon, Meric, 70
Cassirer, Ernst, 66
Castells, Manuel, 25
censorship, 91–3
centres, 33–4, 87–8
Certeau, Michel de, 33
Chaffee, John, 80–1
Chamberlain, Michael, 78–9
Chambers, Robert, 90
Chartier, Roger, 41, 116
China, 8, 27–8, 42, 56–7,
    80–2, 92–3, 101, 115
Christian, David, 123–4
Cicero, 19
Clark, Alice, 122
classification, 29, 54–6, 61–2
Clausewitz, Karl von, 49,
    122
cognitive anthropology, 12
cognitive archaeology, 12,
    124
cognitive history, 123–4
Cohn, Bernard, 37
Colbert, Jean-Baptiste, 24,
    101

collections (see also museums)
    85
Collingwood, Robin G., 65,
    69
colonialism, see empires,
    postcolonialism
comparison, 27, 63–4, 123
Comte, Auguste, 4
concealment, see secrecy
Condorcet, marquis de, 4, 60
constructivism, 116–17
Cook, James, 51, 90
Counter-Reformation, 98–9
crafts, see artisans
Craig, John, 58
criticism, 69, 72–4
Crouch, Nathaniel, 70
cultures of knowledge, 7
curiosity, 17–18
Cuvier, Georges, 63

Darnton, Robert, 25
Darwin, Charles 4, 75
Daston, Lorraine, 45
Descartes, René, 70
description, 58–9, 66
detachment, 46
De Vivo, Filippo, 94
Dewey, Melvil, 31, 55, 62
Diamond, Jared, 22
Diderot, Denis, 95
Dirks, Nicholas, 118
disciplines (see also
    interdisciplinarity), 18–19,
    61
Disciplinierung, 18
displacement, 21, 42, 85–7
dissemination, 77
distance, distanciation, 46
Dreyfus, Alfred, 21
Drucker, Peter, 2, 7
Dumézil, Georges, 63–4
Durkheim, Émile, 41, 70
Dutch East India Company,
    83, 103

East India Company, 36–7, 83, 101
economics, 13, 20, 24–5, 31–2, 43
Edinburgh School, 11
Edison, Thomas, 103
Egypt, 36
Elias, Norbert, 46
Eliot, T. S., 6
Elman, Benjamin, 80–1
embodied knowledge, 38
empires, 14, 32, 35–7, 51, 87, 93, 100
empiricism, 67, 100
encounters, 35, 37, 39
encyclopaedias, 56–7, 91–2, 95–6
epistemology, 10, 66
Erasmus, 97
Euben, Roxanne, 13
evidence, 66–9
examinations, 80–1
exiles, 42–3, 85
expeditions, 50–1
experiments, 67
experts, 31

facts, 47, 69–70
Faust, 18
FBI, 53
Febvre, Lucien, 41, 121
feminism and knowledge, 11, 33, 120
fields of knowledge, 10–11, 19
Fleck, Ludwik, 35, 113
Florida, Richard, 20
Ford Foundation, 24
Foucault, Michel, 7, 10, 13, 26, 29, 33, 35, 84, 98, 102, 109
Fox-Talbot, William, 45,
Free University Berlin, 24
Freud, Sigmund, 49, 65
Fryer, John, 82

Galison, Peter, 45
Galton, Francis, 60
Ganguli, Jadu Nath, 84
Ganjin, 81–2
gatekeepers, 16
Gatrell, Vic, 102
Geertz, Clifford, 65, 75
gender, 119–20
generalist, 21
geography, 12–13, 20, 33, 98, 116
geometrical method, 58
geopolitics of knowledge, 13, 33–4
Gilbert, Geoffrey, 68
Gini, Corrado, 53
Ginzburg, Carlo, 49, 76
global turn, 123
Golinski, Jan, 116
Gorbachev, Mikhail, 96
Greer, Germaine, 121
Guicciardini, Francesco, 74
Gurevich, Aron Y., 119

habitus, 38
Hägerstrand, Torsten, 20
Haraway, Donna, 33, 120
Harrison, Jane, 120
Hastings, Warren, 36
Hawkesworth, John, 90
Heesterman, Jan, 110
heretics, 16
hermeneutics, 64–5
Hernández, Francisco, 50
Higgs, Edward, 102
history, 31, 70–2
history of the book, 5
History of Ideas Club, 23
history of science, 5
Hobbes, Thomas, 40, 58
Hobsbawm, Eric, 40
Holmes, Sherlock, 49
Homer, 73
Horkheimer, Max, 74
Hudson, Liam, 20

Huet, Pierre-Daniel, 58
Huizinga, Johan, 66
Humboldt, Alexander von, 60, 90
Huxley, Aldous, 22

Ibbetson, Agnes, 121
Ibn Battuta, 47
Ibn Jama'a, 79
Ibn Khaldun, 47, 78
iconography, iconology, 65
ignorance, 14, 31–2
imperialism, see empires
implicit knowledge, 37–9
incommensurability, see relativism
India, 36–7, 83–4, 88, 101, 118
information, 6
information age, 25
information overload, 77–8, 115
information society, 4–5
Innis, Harold, 17
innovation, 20–1, 37, 41–2
Institut für Sozialforschung (Institute for Social Research), 23, 43
intellectual property, 13
intellectuals, 21–2, 111–12
interdisciplinarity, 22
interpretation, 64–5
Islamic world, 8, 13, 26, 28

Jacob, Christian, 2, 28
Japan, 82–3, 88, 91–2
Jesuits, 99
Johnson, Samuel, 56
Jones, William, 63, 83
Jowett, Benjamin, 16

Kant, Immanuel, 18, 74
Karam, the, 29
Kenny, Neil, 18
Keynes, John Maynard, 31

Klein, Melanie, 120
Knorr-Cetina, Karin, 117
knowhow, 8, 12, 37–8, 123
knowledge, concepts of, 6–8
knowledge management, 23–5
knowledge society, 4–5, 25
Kuhn, Thomas S., 108–9, 113
Kurosawa, Akira, 76

Labrousse, Ernest, 16, 41
Lachmann, Karl, 73
Landes, David, 122
Lane, Edward William, 36
Latour, Bruno, 12, 34, 117
law, 13, 64–5, 67–9, 74, 76
leaks of information, 94
Leenhardt, Maurice, 82
Le Goff, Jacques, 41, 112
Leibniz, Gottfried Wilhelm, 22, 30, 55
Lelewel, Joachim, 64
Lepetit, Bernard, 41
Lévi-Strauss, Claude, 6–7, 82–3
libraries, librarians, 30–1, 53–5, 115
linguistics, 61, 63
Linnaeus, Carl, 34, 51, 61, 87
Livy, 73
Lloyd, Geoffrey, 27
local knowledge, 13–14, 35, 97, 105–6, 116
Locard, Edmond, 49–50
Locke, John, 68, 71, 85
losing knowledge, 53–4, 115
Lotman, Yuri, 119
Lowe, Robert, 96
Luther, Martin, 95, 97
Lyell, Charles, 4

Mabillon, Jean, 71–2
Macaulay, Thomas, 84, 90
Machlup, Fritz, 24

madrasas, 78–9
management (see also
  knowledge management),
  13, 25
Mannheim, Karl, 10–11, 33–5,
  41, 46, 113
Manning, Bradley (now
  Chelsea Manning), 94
Marchand, Trevor, 38
Marx, Karl, 4, 33
Mauss, Marcel, 70
medicine, 67, 76, 79, 84, 90,
  120
memory, 54, 125
Mencke, Burckhardt, 79–80
Merian, Maria Sybilla, 120
Michelet, Jules, 46
Mignolo, Walter, 13–14,
Mill, John Stuart, 64
missionaries, 42, 81–2
monopolies, 17
Morelli, Giovanni, 49
Mousnier, Roland, 16
Müller, Max, 63, 90
Muhammad, 47, 69
Mulsow, Martin, 7
Mumford, Lewis, 21
museums, 62, 85–6

narration, 74–5
negotiated knowledge, 37, 42
Newton, Isaac, 58
Niebuhr, Barthold, 73
Nonaka, Ikujiro, 13
Nora, Pierre, 2

objectivity, 45
observing, 48–9
orality, 67–8, 78–9, 125
orders of knowledge, 26–8
orientalism, 36
Orta, García de, 88
Ossowski, Stanisław, 35
Otlet, Paul, 55–6

Palgrave, Francis, 52
Panofsky, Erwin, 65
Paracelsus, 79, 95
Paret, Peter, 122
Pareto, Vilfredo, 43
Park, Robert, 43
Pepper, John Henry, 80
erformance, 79–80
peripheries, 33–4, 87–8
Playfair, William, 60
Polanyi, Michael, 22, 37–8
political science, 13
polymath, 21
Popitz, Heinrich, 35
popularization, 89–90
post-colonialism and
  knowledge, 11, 36
Power, Eileen, 121
practices, 28–9
privatization, 97
probability, 68, 71
professionalization, 29–31
proof, 58, 66–9
Propp, Vladimir, 119
psychology, 20
pyrrhonism, 70–1

quantification, 60–1
questionnaires, 99–101, 104
Quintilian, 68

Radolf of Liège, 115
Raginbold of Cologne, 115
Ranke, Leopold von, 31, 46,
  71, 73–4, 110
Rashomon Effect, 76
reformation, 71, 95, 111
regimes of knowledge, see
  orders
relativism, 12, 112–14
Renfrew, Colin, 124
reports, official, 59
Republic of Letters, 86–7
retrieval, 54–6

Ricoeur, Paul, 75
Robertson, William, 68
Rockefeller Foundation, 24

Said, Edward, 11, 36, 84
St Antony's College
Oxford, 24
Salmon, Lucy, 122
Savonarola, Michele, 120
scepticism, 70–1
Schleiermacher,
Friedrich, 65–66
Schlözer, August von, 49
schools, 78, 81, 96
Schumpeter, Joseph, 20
Science Policy Research Unit
(SPRU), 23
scientific revolution, 39, 110
scientification, 18–19, 44
Scott, James C., 13, 105
secrecy, 32, 93–4
Seinsverbundenheit, 10
Selden, John, 69
Shapin, Steven, 66, 110
Shteir, Ann, 121
Simon, Richard, 72
situated knowledge, 10–11,
33–4, 120
Skłodowska-Curie, Marie,
120
Smith, Bonnie, 121
Smith, Dorothy, 100
Smith, Pamela, 39
Snowden, Edward, 94
sociology, 4, 10–11, 32–5,
43, 47, 60, 70, 74,
76–7
Solander, Daniel, 51, 87
Soll, Jacob, 101
Southern, Richard, 115
specialization, 19, 22–3
specialist, 21
Spencer, Herbert, 47, 64
spies, 94

Spinoza, Baruch, 58
Sprat, Thomas, 3, 70
statistics, 49, 53, 60
Stone, Shepard, 24
storage, 52–3
Strickland, Agnes and
Elizabeth, 121
Stukeley, William, 59
styles of thought, 34–6, 41
subjugated knowledges,
35–6

tacit knowledge, 37–9, 123
Tapia, Luis, 14
Tawney, Richard H., 75
think tanks, 27
tools of knowledge, 39–40
traditions, 40–1, 110–11
translation, 41–2, 85, 88–9,
111
Trautmann, Thomas, 84
triumphalism, 114–15
truth, 26, 66

universities, 16–17, 22, 26–7,
48, 57, 61, 79, 83
useful knowledge, 3, 18, 95,
98

Varga, Lucie, 121
Verger, Jacques, 112
verification, 66–9
Verwissenschaftlichung, 18,
44
Vico, Giambattista, 73
VOC, see Dutch East India
Company

Waquet, Françoise, 79
Warburg, Aby, 23, 40
warfare, 49, 98, 122
Weaver, Warren, 24
Weber, Max, 85
Williamson, Alexander, 82

Wissenschaftsgeschichte, 4
Wissensgeschichte, 4
Wissenskulturen, 7
Wissensoziologie, 4
Wolf, Friedrich, 73
Woolf, Virginia, 120

Woolgar, Steve, 117
Worm, Ole, 85
Worsley, Peter, 7
Wower, Johannes, 19

Zola, Émile, 21